W. B. YEATS

Augustine Martin

COLIN SMYTHE
Gerrards Cross, 1990

Copyright © 1983, 1990 by Augustine Martin

First published in 1983

This revised edition first published in 1990
by Colin Smythe Limited, Gerrards Cross, Buckinghamshire

British Library Cataloguing in Publication Data

Martin, Augustine
  W. B. Yeats, 2nd ed.
  1. Poetry in English. Yeats, W. B. (William Butler),
  1865–1939
  I. Title
  821′.8

  ISBN 0–86140–325–8

Produced in Great Britain
Printed and bound by Guernsey Press Co. Ltd.
Vale, Guernsey, C.I.

For my wife, Claire, with love

Contents

1
'Signs of Unusual Genius'

William Butler Yeats was born on 13 June 1865 at 'Georgeville', 5 Sandymount Avenue, Dublin. He was the first of six children to be born to Susan and John Butler Yeats, a young lawyer who, in the first year of his marriage, seemed poised for a triumphant career at the Irish Bar. For the young couple everything looked propitious. Susan Pollexfen, daughter of a rich Sligo shipping family, could look forward to an elegant future in Dublin society where the Yeatses already commanded a wide and distinguished range of acquaintances. Across the road from 'Georgeville' stood Sandymount Castle, home of her husband's maternal uncle, Robert Corbet. Her husband John Butler Yeats had himself inherited an estate at Celbridge, Co. Kildare and a town house in Dorset Street, on the death of his father, Rev. W. B. Yeats, in 1862. There was a net income from the two properties of more than £300 a year. In November 1865 John Butler Yeats impressed and delighted Dublin's men of law with his trenchant inaugural address as auditor of the King's Inns debating society. With his striking good looks, his eloquence, his family connections, he seemed destined for a bright future at the Bar.

But none of this was to be. Sitting as a barrister in the law courts John Butler Yeats discovered the beginnings of another vocation in the skill with which he found himself sketching the faces of his seniors about their daily business. As he sketched he began to feel a distaste for legal practice, what he saw as its pompous triviality and waste of human talent. By the summer of 1886 he had announced to his affronted in-laws at Sligo his intention of going to London to become a

painter. By late July 1867 he and his wife and their two
[2] children — their second, Susan Mary ('Lily'), had been born
at Enniscrone, Co. Sligo the previous August — were settled
uneasily into 23 Fitzroy Road, Regent's Park, London. It was
the first of eight such moves to a new house that the impoverished family was to make over the next ten years, quite apart
from their repeated journeyings on the Pollexfen steamers
back and forth to Sligo for summer holidays. For Susan Yeats
whose unadventurous soul viewed art as a tedious and profitless
mystery it was a disappointment that was to intensify with
each year that passed.

Her husband was in every respect remarkable but most
remarkable in his originality. As a young man he read the
works of Darwin, Comte and John Stuart Mill and was quickly
persuaded to the religious scepticism that was his stance
through life. Yet his rationalism never took precedence over
feeling and imagination. In the wide range of his reading he
prized most of all those passionate utterances in Shakespeare,
Milton, Scott, Shelley, Wordsworth where individual emotion
expressed itself with vehemence and intensity. His sense of
personal uniqueness made him indifferent to the judgement
of society and of the market-place. He believed and constantly
insisted that 'a gentleman is a man not wholly occupied with
getting on' and he consistently strove to ensure that his
children were fulfilled rather than successful. After the manner
of the elder Mill he devoted a great deal of his time to their
education and it was always with the bias of correcting any
tendency towards conformity that might be imposed either
by their schooling, such as it was, or the influence of their
'respectable' and ambitious in-laws, the Pollexfens of Sligo.
He was also remarkable for his improvidence, his bored neglect
of his properties, his virtual inability to complete his pictures
so marvellously begun, his failure ever to make his painting
pay, his guilt-ridden optimism that kept him on his quest for
artistic perfection while his daughters pleaded for credit with
the grocer and the family crowded round a single lamp at
night to conserve lighting oil.

On 23 July 1872 when Willie was seven years old the family went on a summer holiday to Merville, the Pollexfen home at Sligo. The vacation lasted for twenty-eight months and proved crucial for the developing consciousness of the young poet. He fell in love with the landscape and found a growing delight in the fairy lore of his grandfather's servants and the neighbouring cottagers. His cousin, Lucy Middleton, had second sight and the Middleton home at Rosses Point was full of stories of the supernatural and of the sea where the family had made their living respectably as merchant seamen, more remotely and romantically as smugglers. The Middleton house 'Elsinore' was reputed to be haunted and Willie is believed to have seen his first fairy at the window of his bedroom at 'Merville' in 1873. His imagination was constantly stirred by the legendary mountains of Ben Bulben and Knocknarea and when his father read him Scott's 'Lay of the Last Minstrel' by the sea at Rosses Point he conceived 'a wish to turn magician that competed for years with the dream of being killed upon the sea shore'.[1]

Yet his life at Sligo was not altogether happy. He records in his *Autobiographies* that he can 'remember little of childhood but its pain'. At Sligo he was always afraid of his uncles and aunts and he recalls that he 'confused my grandfather with God, for I remember in one of my attacks of melancholy praying that he might punish me for my sins'. Grandfather William Pollexfen was indeed the sort of personality that might make a formative impression on a child so sensitive and insecure as the young W. B. Yeats. The few details chosen by the poet to register that personality are vivid and archetypal: his intimidating silence, his passionate anger, his formidable appearance calculated to 'catch the popular imagination'. William Pollexfen had leaped overboard in the Bay of Biscay to retrieve his hat; he had been honoured by a Spanish town and had never told his wife of it; he had dived beneath a ship of his at the Sligo docks to inspect a fault when his workmen had refused. Willie had seen him whip a crowd of beggars from the yard of 'Merville' after the wedding of his daughter Elizabeth

in 1873. Forty years later when the mature poet recalls and
[4] invokes his ancestors, his 'old fathers', in the volume
Responsibilities, he singles out William Pollexfen as chief
among his exemplars:

> Old merchant skipper that leaped overboard
> After a ragged hat in Biscay Bay;
> You most of all, silent and fierce old man

Though the poet's father never hit it off with his in-laws it
was he who conceded, on the first signs of his son's poetic
talent, that the Pollexfens had 'all the marks of imagination —
the continual absorption in an idea — and that idea never one
of the intellectual or reasoning faculty, but of the affections
and desires and senses. . . . To give them a voice is like giving
a voice to the sea cliffs, when what wild babblings must
break forth'.[2]

Speaking of his own family John B. Yeats had asserted:
'We have ideas but no passions'. The evidence suggests that
he was himself exempt from the deficiency. Apart from his
delight in literary intensity we have the account of both sons
that in the rage of argument with Willie he once challenged
him to stand up and fight and smashed a picture above his
head before leaving the room. This vehemence of character
was to bear heavily on the child's development when John
B. Yeats came to 'Merville' for a visit in the summer of 1873.

The quandary in which the eight-year-old boy was placed
must have been significant if we are to judge by his *Autobiographies*. There he records that he had been 'difficult to
teach' as a child because he had 'found it hard to attend to
anything less interesting than my own thoughts'. His
Pollexfen aunts and uncles had tried to teach him to read
but had failed, concluding that the child — like his inexplic-
able father perhaps — 'had not all his faculties'. The boy
was deeply religious — 'my eyes filling with tears at the
thought of God and of my own sins' — but he hated church
services. Noting that his free-thinking father stayed at home
while the Pollfexens went to Sunday services Willie also

refused to go. It was then that his father gave him his first reading lesson and in the course of it growing 'angry and [5] impatient . . . flung the reading-book' at his pupil's head. The poet, looking back, thought it a ploy on the part of the embarrassed father to get his son back to church. But the reading lessons continued on weekdays and soon conquered the youngster's 'wandering mind'. The religious problem was not so easily disposed of and the poet was eventually to evolve a theological system equally remote from his father's scepticism and the conventional protestantism of the Pollexfens. Part of that system was the fairy faith which he had begun to absorb during this extended visit to Sligo. In February of 1873 his younger brother Bobbie died, aged three, giving the poet his first 'realization of death'. He recalls that his mother and a servant 'had heard the banshee crying the night before he died'. This long and influential visit to Sligo ended in October 1874 when John B. Yeats assembled his family again in London, this time in 14 Edith Villas, Kensington. The memory and the lure of Sligo was to remain a potent element in the poet's consciousness for the rest of his life.

The family's stay at 14 Edith Villas was perhaps the bleakest period of their life together. Into an already crowded household was born a third daughter, Jane Grace, who died ten months later on 6 June 1876. John B. Yeats's career as a portrait painter was still languishing, while the income from the Thomastown estate, managed testily by his uncle Matthew Yeats, had dwindled almost to nothing. His attempt to raise some ready money by the sale of the Dorset Street house in 1877 came to grief, the proceeds being entirely swallowed by the liabilities and expenses. At home Susan became increasingly morose: a bad manager to start with she was defeated by the daily poverty and the constant clamour of tradesmen with demands for payment. The children were unhappy in their overcrowded London home; they lived for their summer holidays at Sligo. Willie grew increasingly troublesome with his fractious Pollexfen temperament and Lolly who shared that temperament grew more aggrieved and difficult with the years;

the sweetness of the Yeatses, shared by Lily, young Jack and their irrepressible father was hard beset to keep a quiet house. The situation was not enhanced when the mercurial artist decided to turn from portrait painting, at which he had by now made a reputation if not a living, to landscapes, which required an entirely new apprenticeship.

John B. Yeats announced his change of direction in Sligo, at the end of his summer vacation 1876 and departed to live with friends, the Earles, at Farnham Royal near Slough in England. Always anxious to counteract the conformist influence of the Sligo aunts he quickly sent for his eldest son to join him. There Willie endured the misery of daily private lessons from his father in geography, chemistry and literature enjoying only his solitary walks through the surrounding countryside. There he observed with significant fascination the progress of one of his father's paintings 'begun in spring and painted all through the year, the picture changing with the seasons' till at last given up unfinished with the appearance of 'snow upon the heath-covered banks'.[3] A stranger in London had once dismissed his father as 'the painter who scrapes out every day what he painted the day before'.[4] Though father and son held each other in unwavering affection and respect through life, the struggle between them was archetypal in its substance, inevitable and relentless in its process. Perhaps it was in a revelation such as this that the son sensed the possibility of facing and coming to terms with this formidable parent.

His sense of his own worth as an 'Irish gentleman' stood him in good stead when he was sent to the Godolphin School, Iffley Road, Hammersmith in the spring of 1877. Three or four years earlier a Sligo aunt had said to him: 'You are going to London. Here you are somebody. There you will be nobody at all'. On his first day at Godolphin he found himself being asked: 'Who's your father? What does he do? How much money has he?' but unlike the young James Joyce at Clongowes he was not intimidated or driven to lies. He had not been encouraged to consider English people superior, 'or over intelligent or well behaved unless they were artists'. Though he was often lonely, estranged and unhappy at school and sometimes victimised by bullies, his father's principles were proof against the bourgeois values of ambition and snobbery that seemed to motivate his classmates: 'I remind myself that I am an artist's son and must take some work as the whole end of life and not think as the others do of becoming well off and living pleasantly'.[5]

His scholastic record at Godolphin was undistinguished. A school report for 1887 shows him twenty-first out of a class of thirty-one. In English he is nineteenth and 'very poor in spelling', a weakness that persisted through his greatest literary productions. The summer report of 1878 placed him sixteenth in a class of twenty-one with comments like 'bad', 'exceedingly weak', 'very indifferent' and an unexpected 'good' for Latin and conduct. John B. Yeats took the report to mean that his son was 'amiable but hopeless' but he was not depressed. Headmasters, he believed, were interested only in 'head boys' and thought of the others 'only when they break the rules'. He was satisfied with the boy's intellectual progress at home where he 'learned to believe in art and poetry and the sovereignty of intellect and of the spirit'. His low opinion of headmasters did not, however, prevent him from rejoicing when his son, in his last year at Godolphin, was declared 'of exceptional ability' in science. At that 'blessed phrase' he found himself exclaiming 'he will be a man of science; it is great to be a man of science'.[6] It was thus, on a chord of literary failure and scientific excellence that the future poet and necromancer completed his formal schooling in England with the Lent term of 1881.

Before their return to Ireland in that year the family had a comparatively serene interlude when they moved in the spring of 1879 to a new house at 8 Woodstock Road, Bedford Park. The Bedford Park estate had been designed, amid great celebrity, as a sort of artists' colony by Norman Shaw. For the young poet the prospect of Bedford Park was 'a romantic excitement' and though it did not turn out to be the walled

city that his father's descriptions had conjured up, it delighted
[8] his imagination with its trees, its winding streets, its 'beautiful
houses, the houses of artists and the dining room of his
dancing mistress's house 'where Sinbad the sailor might have
sat'.[7] The romance of this garden city transcended the bleak-
ness of the Yeats's domestic situation. Conceived of a sense
of beauty and peopled by artists it may have been the
beginning of the poet's life-long meditation on the ideal
human city, revived by his later visit to Urbino and his study
of Blake, in images of Phidias's Athens and his own visionary
Byzantium. When Yeats returned to London as a young man
in 1887 his first recorded impression was of the city's ugliness.

> Everything had become to me a form of ethics, and as I
> walked the streets I used to believe that I could define
> exactly the bad passion or moral vacancy that had created,
> after centuries, every detail of architectural ugliness . . .
> the size, the oppressive weight of the new Law Courts
> made me miserable for an afternoon.[8]

That was after a sojourn of five and a half years in Ireland
where the family moved from Bedford Park towards the end
of 1881.

John B. Yeats moved to Dublin in the summer of 1881
and rented a studio at 44 York Street near St Stephen's
Green. Towards the end of the year, when the lease on their
house at Bedford Park had expired, he moved the family to
Balscadden Cottage near the seaside village of Howth on the
northern edge of Dublin Bay. There the family, and Willie
in particular, entered upon one of the sunniest periods of
their life. With the sea, the open sky and the fishing community Susan Yeats recovered much of the vivacity which had
attracted her husband to her seventeen years before in Sligo.
When the family moved in 1882 to Island View, a cottage by
by the harbour, she would spend hours talking to the servant
'on the only themes outside our house that seemed of interest —
the fishing-people of Howth, or the pilots and fishing-people
of Rosses Point'. 'She read no books, but she and the fisher-

man's wife would tell each other stories that Homer might have told, pleased with any moment of sudden intensity and laughing together over any point of satire.' The few glimpses that we get of Susan Yeats in this Howth setting dramatise the pathos of her life. Her element was nature and the harmonious ways of simple people, yet it was her destiny to live mostly in an alien city and a household obsessed with art and intellect.

The poet's recollections of Howth are of its romance and adventure. His life-long dream of crossing water to enchanted islands and cities may have had its roots in his daring boating excursions to Lambay Island, or in the reveries awoken by his taking the glass out of his window 'so that in stormy weather the spray would soak my bed at night'. In an early anecdote, 'Village Ghosts', which he based on his mother's chat with the servant, he recalls Howth's shape and atmosphere, 'its crooked lanes, its old abbey churchyard full of grass, its green background of small fir trees, and its quay, where lie a few tarry fishing-luggers'.[10]

Science had not yet surrendered to poetry, so he found much to interest him in the rock formations, the flora and fauna of the area. He recalls that he had by then read 'Darwin and Wallace, Huxley and Haeckel, and would spend hours plaguing a pious geologist who . . . came with a hammer to look for fossils in the Howth Cliffs' by attacking Ussher's chronology of the world's history. But one can sense the poet gaining the ascendant over the scientist when he writes of 'a certain rare moth fluttering along the edges of the tide, just at the end of evening or the beginning of dawn'.

Every morning Willie took the train to Dublin with his father, breakfasted with him at his York Street studio and proceeded to the Erasmus Smith High School, Harcourt Street, where he was to attend for the next three and a half years. One could hardly imagine a more stimulating environment for adolescent genius. At the studio he met and conversed with such friends of his father as Edward Dowden, Shakespearean critic and Professor of English at Trinity College, and Sarah Purser, artist and wit, whose acerbic humour made her respected and feared throughout a city legendary for its malice.

[10] If they had no friends in for breakfast father and son recited poetry before Willie went to school and John B. to his easel. Neither activity prospered in the conventional way. The forty-two year old artist, plagued by his inability to finish a portrait, failed to earn a living, while his son, still finding it hard to 'attend to anything less interesting than my thoughts', endured the routine of classwork without pleasure or satisfaction: 'I had begun to think of my school work as an interruption of my natural history studies . . . and what could I, who never worked when I was not interested, do with a history lesson that was but a column of seventy dates? I was worst of all at literature, for we read Shakespeare for his grammar exclusively'.[12] In later life he regretted that his father had not taken him away from school and educated him personally: 'He would have taught me nothing but Greek and Latin, and I would now be a properly educated man, and would not have to look in useless longing at books that have been, through the poor mechanism of translation, the builders of my soul, nor to face authority with the timidity born of excuse and evasion.'[13]

Timidity is not among the qualities recalled by his teachers and classmates at High School. One of the masters, John McNeill, remembers Yeats as 'dark and good-looking and a thoroughly good boy . . . showing at every turn signs of unusual genius'. The Reverend F. R. Montgomery Hitchcock recalls a 'gentlemanly dreamy fellow . . . a good talker' who would 'argue and discuss matters with the master' and who would 'spout reams of poetry to us, which none of us could comprehend, as his delivery was so fast . . . really a charming fellow, rather fond of attitudinizing'. His younger contemporary, W. K. Magee — later, under the pen-name 'John Eglinton' to be his companion in letters and mysticism — recalled him as 'yellow skinned, lank, loose coated' with the 'beginnings of a beard'. Another of his fellows describes him as a 'queer chap' with 'something quietly repellant in his manner which affected even his relations with the masters'.[14]

One can sense even through these few and apparently contrary impressions the individuality which his father had always [11] encouraged, coupled, perhaps, with the insecurity of a youth who knew that he could never compete with these orthodox and ambitious products of an educational system that placed examinations as the supreme goal of scholastic endeavour.

By High School's standards Yeats was a comparative failure. He declined to sit the Intermediate Examination or the scholarship examinations to the university. Therefore, unlike his father and grandfather he did not go to Trinity College. This was due primarily to his uneven academic record; partly perhaps, to his developing sense of a different vocation and destiny. Gradually and to the mild dismay of his father Willie conceived an antagonism to Edward Dowden and to the Trinity intellectual establishment which he thought Dowden represented. Dowden, for instance, had no feeling for Irish nationalism. The elder Yeats could, in the generosity of his affection, overlook this, but his uncompromising son could only see it as part of an ambivalence if not actual hypocrisy in Dowden's character. Willie, used to his father's enthusiasm and intellectual frankness, resented Dowden's caution and reserve. The gap between the two men was to widen with the years. Though Dowden was to prove both shrewd and appreciative of the younger man's work he remained studiously aloof from the movement in Irish poetry of which Yeats was soon to become leader. When Willie found a mentor in the old Fenian, John O'Leary, Dowden and the 'West-Briton' mentality which he was seen to represent provided an ideal target and antagonist for the young man's polemical and combative instincts. Thus, while his hero Oscar Wilde had made his rapid way upwards through the path of Trinity scholarship and expatriate fame, Yeats himself chose to build his singing school of Irish materials, outside the walls of academe.

John B. Yeats believed that every child should have some schooling in art. When his son finished at Harcourt Street in 1883 he was entered as a student at the Metropolitan

School of Art, Kildare Street. A move that might have helped [12] him out from under his father's shadow seems for a time to have intensified that formidable influence. No matter how hard he tried at the easel for a 'deliberate' style he found 'I could only imitate my father'. In reaction, perhaps, he began to cultivate a personal manner 'walking with artificial stride in memory of Hamlet' – whom he had seen Irving play – and pausing to observe in the shop windows his 'tie gathered into a loose sailor-knot and to regret that it could not be always blown out by the wind like Byron's tie in the picture'.[15] It was at the art school that he met the Ulster poet, painter and mystic, George Russell who was soon to take the pseudynom 'A.E.' and to exert such a powerful influence on a generation of Irish artists and writers. Russell was in the strict sense a visionary and his visions, especially of the old Celtic gods and of the Irish fairies, were to absorb and inspire Yeats to a new concept of art and reality for more than a decade.

Russell's influence was buttressed by Yeats's reading A. P. Sinnett's *Esoteric Buddhism* which his aunt Isabella Pollexfen sent him in 1884. When he lent Sinnett's book to his brilliant schoolmate, Charles Johnston, the result was the Hermetic Society which had its first meeting on 15 June 1885. At last William had found the means of escaping his father's intellectual dominance. Indeed his growing commitment to mysticism, spiritualism and magic was to prove a fierce and often painful source of argument and division between father and son. It was this that almost brought them to blows in the poet's London bedroom some years later. The father's distress is understandable: that a boy brought up on the best Comptean principles of scientific and rational thought should seem to surrender his intelligence to visionary superstition, to a world far less intellectually respectable than Canterbury or even Rome, was something that John B. Yeats struggled to understand throughout his life. But to the son it was more than a symbolic bridgehead established to counter his parent's influence. What we may call the mystical way – involving Hermetism, Theosophy, Cabbalism, magic, the Vedas combined in varying proportions at different stages of his life — became his chief means of apprehending the world, of [13] bringing the discords of his complex nature into unity. It became the formal basis of his art, enabling him to find a tradition of thought going back to Plotinus and Plato through Baudelaire, Balzac, Coleridge, Swedenborg, Boehme, Bruno and Joachim of Flora. This underground church, devoted to the visionary imagination, was a powerful counter-force both to the sanctioned Christianity of the day and the scientific atheism of his father. Years later, in a statement that has since become a favourite with Yeatsian scholars, he describes how art and mysticism combined to rescue him from the spiritual dilemma of his early manhood.

> I was unlike others of my generation in one thing only. I am very religious, and deprived by Huxley and Tyndall, whom I detested, of the simple minded-religion of my childhood, I had made a new religion, almost an infallible Church of poetic tradition, of a fardel of stories, and of personages, and of emotions, inseparable from their first expression, passed on from generation to generation by poets and painters with some help from philosophers and theologians.[16]

At one stroke he had found a mode of thought which was equally opposed to the protestantism of his aunts and the scientific rationalism of his father. The future disciple of Blake had already refused to be enslaved in another man's system by founding his own.

The Dublin to which the Yeatses returned in 1881 was the centre of political turbulence arising from the battle between Parnell and Davitt on the one hand and the British Government on the other over Home Rule and the Land League agitation for agrarian reform. Within four years the Ashbourne Act of 1885 was to provide the means by which the Irish tenant farmers could buy out their holdings from the landlords. John Butler Yeats, whose career as an absentee landlord had been only marginally more lucrative than his career in portraiture, was one of the first landlords to avail himself of [14] the new arrangements. He managed the sale of the Thomastown estate with such characteristic incompetence that he gained scarcely a shilling from the transaction.

The prelude to the Ashbourne Act had been confused and violent and the Yeatses had had a vivid initiation. Side by side with the constitutional agitation of Parnell and Davitt the secret and revolutionary Irish Republican Brotherhood — lineal descendant of the Fenians — was at work, together with more desperate apostles of physical force such as the Invincibles. Parnell himself had been imprisoned and on his release in May 1882 the infamous Phoenix Park murders were carried out by the Invincibles. The new Chief Secretary, Lord Frederick Cavendish, with the unpopular Under-Secretary Thomas Burke, were stabbed to death within view of the Viceregal Lodge, indeed, under the eyes of the new Lord Lieutenant who saw the attack but could not recognise the victims at that distance. On the day of the murders Lily and Lolly welcome for the new Lord Lieutenant. Next morning they Yeats passed through a Dublin festooned with tributes of went to Church with their Uncle Matthew and heard the murders denounced from the pulpit. A repressive Crimes Bill was passed at Westminster and the years that followed, tense with intrigue and controversy, provided an ideal forcing-house for the young poet's political intelligence.

2
'All Dreams and Gentleness'

In 1884 the Yeats family, still dogged by poverty, moved from their happy home at Howth to 10 Ashfield Terrace, Harold's Cross, an uninspiring suburb on the south side of the city. Willie, now aged nineteen, had settled upon a career in literature. His habit of reciting his compositions becomes a feature, if not a trial, to his hard-pressed family, clustered around a single lamp in the living room: 'Then his sisters would call out to him, "Now Willie, stop composing!"' And he would meekly lower his voice. 'Visitors to the house would awake at night to hear the young poet intoning his verses in the darkness. The sense of a voice speaking was to persist through his life-work in prose and poetry. It is significant that his first published poems were dramatic. They appeared in March 1885.

The suburban setting, a source of depression to Mrs Yeats, had its compensations for father and son. They could now breakfast with Dowden at his nearby residence in Rathgar. In the evenings they could enter more fully into the social and political life of the city. A favourite resort was the Contemporary Club, founded by Charles Hubert Oldham at Trinity College from which it moved to Ponsonby's Bookshop in Grafton Street in 1885. Though its founder was an ardent Home Ruler there was a clause forbidding the club to take any political action. It met to discuss 'the social, political, and literary questions of the day'. John B. Yeats became a member and for the next two years the young poet accompanied him to its meetings. Here among such personalities as Douglas Hyde, Michael Davitt, Thomas W. H. Rolleston and John F. Taylor, the twenty-year-old writer, in the cut and thrust of debate, formed those convictions about Irish nationalism that were to underpin his thought for life. There he developed those skills in rhetoric which were to serve him so well on public platform and private committee through his active career. There also he met John O'Leary and fell permanently under his spell. Before the year was out his career as poet and man of letters was busily under way.

It is not hard to see why Yeats was drawn to John O'Leary. It was part of his character to look for exemplars among his elders: the magnetic pull of his father, Dowden and his grandfather had already inspired, intimidated and challenged him. O'Leary with his striking appearance – his 'noble head' remains one of the 'beautiful lofty things' celebrated in the later poetry – his twenty years of imprisonment and exile, his dignified sense of patriotism, his devotion to cultural nationality rather than militant nationalism, all held an obvious attraction for the younger man. More especially O'Leary was of native Catholic stock and thus supplied a dimension that had so far been missing from Yeats's pantheon of elders. The old Fenian embodied a sense of Ireland older and more indigenous than that of Dowden, Pollexfen or the Yeatses themselves. He stood for 'Romantic Ireland', ancient, mysterious and resurgent, what Yeats in his final poems termed the 'indomitable Irishry'. O'Leary seems to have been the ruling presence at the Contemporary Club after his return from exile in 1885. Around him the debate on Republicanism, Home Rule, Unionism, physical force, agrarian reform, literary tradition, religious and socialist theory swirled and eddied. The elder Yeats frequently joined in the debate but more often contented himself with sketching the combatants. The younger hurled himself with courage and verve into the centre of controversy. It was soon clear that he stood out, despite his years, as the chief opponent of John F. Taylor, a lawyer of vehement Catholic and nationalist convictions, regarded as the most able orator of his time in Dublin. Yeats's views on art and 'supernaturalism' ran counter to Taylor's orthodoxies and their temperaments seem to have been

naturally designed for collision. In his 'Reveries over Childhood and Youth' Yeats recalls hearing an account of a great [17]
speech on the Irish language that Taylor had given at Trinity —
a speech which so hit the popular imagination that Joyce
included his version of it in the Aeolus episode of *Ulysses*. The
poet recalls: 'I braved Taylor again and again as one might a
savage animal as a test of courage, but always found him worse
than my expectation.' Yet he is pleased when Taylor meets
him in a London street and says: 'Yeats . . . if you and . . .
[naming another adversary] were born in a small Italian
principality in the Middle Ages, he would have friends at Court
and you would be in exile with a price on your head.'

The practice of debate helped to develop in Yeats a tendency
of mind that proved basic in his poetic method — the testing
of truth by opposition and antithesis. He was later to say that
out of the struggle with others came rhetoric, out of the
struggle with ourselves came poetry. But the struggle itself,
the antinomy, was always crucial, the opposition of man and
mask, self and antiself, the creative mind registering thesis
and antithesis in a perpetual exchange and renewal of energy
and insight.

It was at the Contemporary Club too that Yeats began to
discover the ardour and complexity with which concepts of
nationalism, religion, history and politics were entertained,
exercised and defined in the Irish context. In this volatile
political climate art could not live by art alone. O'Leary
deemed it necessary to advise the fledgling poet that he must
have either the priests or the nationalists on his side in order
to succeed. With the same breath O'Leary declared Yeats
the only young Contemporary 'who would ever be reckoned
a genius'. In later life the poet declared that 'From these
debates, from O'Leary's conversation, and from the Irish
books he lent or gave me has come all that I have set my hand
to since'.[17]

Early in 1885 Oldham founded the *Dublin University
Review* and in its March issue two lyrics 'Song of the Fairies'
and 'Voices' by W. B. Yeats mark the young poet's first

appearance in print. In the April and July issues he published
[18] his extended poetic drama *The Island of Statues* which he later
describes as 'an Arcadian play in imitation of Edmund
Spenser'. The piece had already been approved after the poet
had read it aloud at Oldham's rooms in Trinity.

The play dramatises a theme that persists with Yeats, in
different forms, throughout his creative career. The hero and
heroine of the drama find the means of bringing back to life
beings who have been turned to statues through the work of an
enchantress. The creatures, faced with the choice of life in
Arcadia or the real world opt for Arcadia, thus foreshadowing
Innisfree, Oisin's islands, and Byzantium's artifice of eternity.
The play's publication is the culmination of his early efforts at
verse drama — *Vivien and Time* and *Mosada* were both written
in 1884.

While it is not a successful play *The Island of Statues* is
clearly the work of a genuine poet. Its epilogue, re-named 'The
Song of the Happy Shepherd' with only a few revisions, has
stood as the opening to his *Collected Poems* since its definitive
form in 1933. His rejection of Darwin's 'grey truth' and his
pleas for imaginative vision can hardly have been lost on his
proud and perplexed father whose own aesthetic doctrines
and artistic labour had brought so few tangible rewards:

> The woods of Arcady are dead,
> And over is their antique joy;
> Of old the world on dreaming fed;
> Grey Truth is now her painted toy;

His twentieth year continued to be a momentous one for
Yeats. Mohini Chatterji, a Brahmin disciple of Madame
Blavatsky, came to Dublin at the invitation of the Hermetic
Society and gave the poet advice that became the substance
of a poem written almost half a century later:

> I asked if I should pray,
> But the Brahmin said,
> 'Pray for nothing, say

Every night in bed,
'I have been a king
I have been a slave,
Nor is there anything,
Fool, rascal, knave,
That I have not been,
And yet upon my breast
A myriad heads have lain

More felicitous and prophetic advice for the poet would be hard to imagine as he set out towards his chameleon destiny.

Meanwhile one of his happiest and most valuable relationships was with the Catholic poetess, Katharine Tynan. The friendship extended to the two families, the Yeats sisters enjoying the hospitality of the Tynan farmhouse at Clondalkin and Katharine visiting at John B. Yeats's studio and spending nights at Harold's Cross where her sleep was frequently disturbed by Willie's nocturnal declamations. To her he was 'all dreams and gentleness . . . beautiful to look at with his dark face, its touch of vivid colouring, the night black hair, the eager dark eyes . . . he lived, breathed, ate, drank and slept poetry'. Her admiration for his intellectual judgment was shrewd and accurate: 'he had an uncanny way of standing aside and looking at the game of life as a spectator. . . . Heaven knows what rubbish he delivered us from! We were all writing like poets of a country newspaper'.[18] Katharine Tynan's influence on Yeats was considerable and salutary. When she suggested that he should choose a poetic theme from Irish legend he embarked upon his first successful long poem *The Wanderings of Oisin* which was published to acclaim in 1889. She was present in 1886 at Yeats's first seance where he seems to have been so possessed by the attendant spirits that he was frightened away from spiritualism for more than a decade. When later he suggested marriage to her and was gently turned down his reaction seems to have been one of mild relief. Her memoirs *Twenty Five Years* (1913) and *The Middle Years* (1916) shed valuable light on Yeats's mind during this formative period.

In 1886 John B. Yeats having failed to make his mark as a
[20] professional portrait painter in Dublin returned to London
and took on a rented house at 58 Eardley Crescent, South
Kensington. With the family, who moved reluctantly and in
stages it was a most unhappy decision. For Willie it was
especially unwelcome as he had begun to dig himself firmly
into the intellectual life of Dublin. On 9 August Samuel
Ferguson had died giving him the ideal platform for a mani-
festo of poetic faith and creative intent. Yeats was provoked
by the terms and tone of the obituaries especially by Mahaffy's
remark in the *Athenean* that though Ferguson knew the 'real
grievances of his country . . . yet there was never a more loyal
or orderly British citizen'. Yeats begins his article by taking
Dowden to task for failing as a critic to give Ferguson the
support of his immense prestige. If Ferguson had written for
the glory of that 'more than dubious achievement British
Civilisation, the critics, probably including Professor Dowden,
would have taken care of his reputation'. But because
Ferguson served his country's heritage and 'restored to our
hills and rivers their epic interest' he has been slighted and
rejected by the 'West-Briton' Trinity Establishment. In
vindicating Ferguson's achievement Yeats places himself firmly
in the line of succession: 'The nation has found in Davis a
battle call, as in Mangan its cry of despair; but he only, the
one Homeric poet of our time, could give us immortal companions still wet with the dew of their primal world'.[19]

In this sentence Yeats finds his identity as a poet: he is
defining Anglo-Irish literature as a tradition separate from that
of Tennyson and the English Victorians. In his two Ferguson
essays of 1886 — the lesser piece was for *The Irish Fireside* —
he dwells at length on the older poet's skill with folk ballad
and epic recension, detailing the poems in which Ferguson's
merits most clearly appear. Within the year he had written
a short epic on the legendary King Goll and one of his best
folk lyrics, 'The Stolen Child'. In March 1887 he published
an essay in appreciation of James Clarence Mangan and in
September of the following year an essay in praise of William

Allingham 'The Poet of Ballyshannon'. Through O'Leary's influence he was taken on by the *Providence Sunday Journal* [21] and John Boyle O'Reilly's *The Boston Pilot* as an Irish literary correspondent. Calling himself the 'Celt' Yeats brought the good news of an Irish literary revival to a converted if variously informed Irish-American readership, to whom he preached the importance of national culture and the need for a de-Anglicised homeland. It was therefore a logical step that he should begin his long Irish poem *The Wanderings of Oisin* which was to be the title poem of his first published volume of poetry in 1889. He is firmly on the path towards his formal declaration of literary intent in 'To Ireland in the Coming Times' (1893) when he proclaims

> Know that I would accounted be
> True brother of a company
>
> That sang, to sweeten Ireland's wrong
> Ballad and story, rann and song. . . .
>
> Nor may I less be counted one
> With Davis, Mangan, Ferguson,

By May 1887 Yeats had joined his family and his letters are full of distress with 'this horrid . . . this dreadful London' where he feels as great an exile as Robinson Crusoe. The family life at Eardley Crescent was beset with miseries from the start. The house was small and ugly. Susan Yeats, ill and dispirited, tried to make a home of it while her husband went to Oxford on one of his rare portrait commissions. First Lily fell ill and then Susan suffered her first stroke. Later in the year both moved to Derby, near Huddersfield, to recuperate at the home of a Pollexfen relative. The family longed for a return to the garden city of Bedford Park which had cheered their last period in London. The following year their luck was in. On 24 March 1888 John B. Yeats moved into 3 Blenheim Road, Bedford Park with Willie, Jack and his younger daughter, Lolly. His wife and Lily joined them on 13 April. Though they remained desperately poor their spirits revived with the beauty of the house, the friendliness and colour of the neighbourhood. Willie writes elatedly to Katharine Tynan of 'a fine roomy house, which by good luck we have got very cheap. Bedford Park is the least Londonish place hereabouts, a silent tree-filled place where everything is a little idyllic ... I will have a study to myself with one of those white balconies native to that part of the world.'

The cosmopolitan atmosphere was a salutary antidote to the Irish provincialism that had in fact limited the vision of Mangan, Davis and Ferguson. The distance from Dublin afforded Yeats a perspective on Irish nationalism. His love of Sligo was intensified by his fierce longing to go back which he did yearly through the decade. Meanwhile London was alive with intellectual stimulation. Within the immediate vicinity lived a wide circle of his father's friends. The Irish poet and playwright John Todhunter lived nearby; his play *A Sicilian Idyll* was performed at the Bedford Park Clubhouse in 1890. Edwin Ellis was a constant visitor and Yeats collaborated with him on the three-volume edition of Blake that appeared in 1893. W. E. Henley, poet and editor of the *Scots Observer* attracted to his house writers as disparate as Oscar Wilde – whom Yeats met there – Robert Louis Stevenson and Rudyard Kipling. Wilde asked Yeats to Christmas dinner in 1888, apparently in the belief that the younger man was alone in London, a fiction in which Yeats was happy to acquiesce. After dinner Wilde read to him from his essay, 'The Decay of Lying', introducing him to the notion of masks which Yeats was later to adapt and develop into a coherent aesthetic theory. Among the visitors to the Yeats household were T. W. Rolleston and G. K. Chesterton, who thought Willie 'the best talker I have ever met, except his father'.

Another centre of intellectual energy was the house of William Morris whose romances had a deep influence on Yeats's work. Among those he welcomed to his drawing room to talk of socialism and art was Bernard Shaw and his temporary mistress Florence Farr, Mrs Emery, the beautiful actress who was eventually to come to Dublin and play in Yeats's *The Countess Cathleen*. Later Yeats himself was to be her lover 'until she got bored with him', but she remained his friend for the rest of her life. She studied embroidery and weaving together with the Yeats sisters in the workshop of Morris's sister, May. It was there that Lolly and Lily acquired the skills which enabled them to found the Dun Emer and Cuala industries when the family returned again to Dublin in 1902.

In the Rhymers Club, founded by the Welsh writer and editor Ernest Rhys, Yeats moved among his younger contemporaries. The group met weekly at the Cheshire Cheese, Fleet Street, a pub with an upstairs room where they could read aloud their most recent compositions and discuss literature. Among those who attended were Arthur Symons, poet and critic of French symbolism, Ernest Dowson, poet and creator of 'Cynara' and Lionel Johnson, Anglo-Irish poet and Catholic mystic. Their characters inform Yeats's long poem 'The Grey Rock' published twenty years later and are the subject of a vivid chapter of his *Autobiographies*, 'The Tragic Generation'. Closely allied to these 'companions of the Cheshire Cheese' was Aubrey Beardsley, editor of the *Yellow Book*, which fell foul of public opinion when the Wilde scandal broke. Its successor, *The Savoy*, sustained the tradition of 'decadence' under the more temperate editorship of Symons. Yeats contributed to both journals, somewhat to the scandal of his more conservative friends. With the painter Charles Ricketts he was loyal to Beardsley when a campaign of slander — accusing him wrongly of homosexuality — was levelled against him. Ricketts and Yeats were constant visitors to the bedside of Mabel Beardsley, his sister, in her final illness. Yeats's exquisite elegy, 'Upon a Dying Lady' captures the pathos, wit and extravagance of their mood and time.

From the beginning of the decade Yeats was building up a busy if not very remunerative practice as a freelance literary journalist. His steadiest work came from *The Boston Pilot* whose editor John Boyle O'Reilly knew O'Leary and had a lively interest in Irish cultural developments. Yeats's contributions to the newspaper were published in volume form together with his articles in *The Providence Journal* in *Letters*

to the New Island in 1934. They chart vividly the development
of his thoughts on literature, culture and nationality between 1889 and 1892. A glance at the list of his contributions to newspapers and journals would suggest enormous energy even in one who had not the central commitment to the creation of great art that Yeats had. When he thought of accepting permanent work as assistant editor on a newspaper his father was quick to dissuade him, as he confides in a letter to Katharine Tynan – first in a long line of *confidantes*:

> To me the hope of regular work is a great thing, for it would mean more peace of mind than I have had lately, but Papa sees all kinds of injury to me in it. It makes him quite sad. Perhaps the loss of mental liberty entailed in routine is always harmful. On the other hand it would save me from the insincerity of writing on all kinds of subjects, of writing on other men's truth.

He stuck to his literary piece-work, labouring in the British Museum to produce seven separate books as editor before the turn of the century – collections of tales, stories and poems including selections from Carleton and the Irish novelists as well as the massive edition of Blake in collaboration with Ellis. The work was ill paid, but it brought his name before the public, while the research into Ireland's nineteenth century and the mind of Blake fed constantly into his own original work through the decade.

While trying to complete *The Wanderings of Oisin* Yeats seems to have come close to nervous collapse. His letters record an acute sense of crisis: 'I had one of my collapses, having done over-much reading lately – I suppose – I walk much of the way to the British Museum. . . . I thought I was in for a considerable collapse but it wore off. I could only speak with difficulty at first.' It is probable that the young poet's susceptibility to nervous exhaustion was partly due to sexual frustration. The *Memoirs* – not published till 1972 – constantly link his sense of failure in money matters and in literary output with his sexual timidity and inexperience.

I had much trouble with my senses, for I am not naturally chaste. . . . My struggle with my senses made me dread the [25] subject of sex, and I always tried to change the subject when Ellis began any of his stories and reminiscences, and was often made uncomfortable by Mrs Ellis who, because I was very delicate, assumed I was living a dissipated life. Once, when York Powell began to show some friends, among whom I was, caricatures of the night life of Paris by some famous French artist, I left the table and walked up and down at the end of the room. Yet women filled me with curiosity and my mind seemed never long to escape from the disturbance of my senses. . . . And I added to the almost unendurable strain of my senses a conviction that I was without industry and without will.[20]

It is therefore understandable that *The Wanderings of Oisin* (1889) should have had to suffer the repeated charge of escapism, ethereality, vagueness and inconclusiveness of theme and language. Oisin, son of Finn, accompanies his fairy lover, Niamh, through the Isle of Dancing, the Isle of Battles and the Isle of Forgetfulness. Nowhere does Oisin find the Isle of Content. And despite the hero's boastings to Patrick of 'the white body that lay by mine' the poem conveys no sense of erotic fulfilment. Indeed its two most typical images are the 'hornless deer' chased by a 'phantom hound' and the lady with 'an apple of gold in her tossing hand' pursued forever by a 'beautiful young man' with 'quenchless gaze and fluttering hair'. Writing to Katharine Tynan Yeats declares that 'the whole poem is full of symbols' to which only he 'has the key'. 'The romance is for my readers', he goes on, 'they must not know there is a symbol anywhere.' Seen against the evidence of his life the dominant symbolism is that of erotic longing and frustration, a fact recognised by the poet in old age when he wrote 'The Circus Animal's Desertion':

First that sea-rider Oisin led by the nose
Through three enchanted islands, allegorical dreams,
Vain gaiety, vain battle, vain repose,

Themes of the embittered heart, or so it seems,
That might adorn old songs or courtly shows;
But what cared I that set him on to ride,
I, starved for the bosom of his faery bride?

Yeats knew the human limitation that lay behind the poetic achievement. With startling self-knowledge he confides to Katharine Tynan that he is writing 'not the poetry of insight and knowledge, but of longing and complaint – the cry of the heart against necessity. I hope some day to alter that and write the poetry of insight and knowledge.' This self-criticism was uttered in March 1988, just before he met Maud Gonne who was to intensify rather than resolve his difficulty. She called on the house at Bedford Park with an introduction from John O'Leary.

> I had never thought to see in a living woman so great beauty. It belonged to famous pictures, to poetry, to some legendary past. A complexion like the blossom of apples, and yet the face and body had the beauty of lineaments which Blake calls the highest beauty because it changes least from youth to age, and a stature so great that it seemed of a divine race.[21]

Maud inspired him through a lifetime of great love poetry and unrequited passion. She refused all his offers of marriage with the cruel but accurate reflection that the pain of his longing would convert itself into poetry to poetry. With her secret love for the French patriot Millevoye — whose illegitimate child she had secretly borne — her passion for social revolution and Irish nationalism, her insensitive political alliance with John F. Taylor, Yeats's enemy, her abstracted concern for humanitarian causes rather than for the poet's immediate agony, she drove him close to the edge of psychic breakdown. In his *Memoirs* he records bitterly that his friends 'had all mistresses of one kind or another and that most, at need, went home with harlots ... I had never since childhood kissed a woman's lips. At Hammersmith I saw a woman of the town walking up and

and down in the empty railway station. I thought of offering myself to her, but the old thought came back, "no, I love the [27] most beautiful woman in the world".'

Relief and fulfilment came in the form of a beautiful English woman, Olivia Shakespear a cousin of Lionel Johnson — referred to in his writings as Diana Vernon. He first met her at a literary dinner in 1894 and was struck by her 'incomparable distinction'. He wrote to her from Sligo and later, when they had become lovers, she told him that these 'were unconscious love-letters', and he was 'taken by surprise at the description'. For him her beauty, 'dark and still, had the nobility of defeated things'.[22] In 1895 he moved out of Bedford Park to take rooms with his friend Arthur Symons at Fountain Court. The following year he moved to Woburn Buildings in Bloomsbury to make possible his affair with Olivia. They had first thought to confess their passion to her husband, an elderly solicitor, but then thought it kinder to deceive him. The affair, tactfully and tenderly recorded in the *Memoirs*, seems to have healed the wound of Yeats's sexual loneliness and enriched his life incomparably. Though their intimacy lasted only a year — the shadow of Maud fell between them — their friendship lasted through life. He had remarkable skill in retaining his lovers as friends, and an especial gift for the friendship of brilliant women — Olivia, Maud, Katharine Tynan, Florence Farr, Lady Gregory, Dorothy Wellesley. A late lyric recalls the affair with Olivia Shakespear, its excitement, sensuality and risk:

A mermaid found a swimming lad,
Picked him for her own,
Pressed her body to his body,
Laughed; and plunging down
Forgot in cruel happiness
That even lovers drown.

Meanwhile Yeats's interest in the mystical and occult was advancing along its curious path. Within months of his return to London, in June 1887, he was initiated into a group called the Hermetic Students at a studio in Charlotte Street. Madame Blavatsky had taken up residence in London that year and Yeats soon became part of her circle. This intriguing woman had published her first book, *Isis Unveiled* in 1877, outlining her elaborate system of theosophical belief, which she later expanded in her monumental *The Secret Doctrine*. In an age disturbed by the discoveries of Darwin and dissatisfied with the narrowness of Victorian religion and morality Blavatsky's weird but all-inclusive scheme of belief had an understandable success. She had travelled extensively in the East and claimed intimacy with learned Mahatmas in Tibet. She argued that western religion and western science were corrupt distortions of an ancient authentic doctrine that embraced science, art and religion. It postulated seven 'rounds' or levels of existence for the human soul, our earthly state being the fourth. Progress upward to the seventh round was one of increasing spirituality eventually reaching nirvana, absolute union with the Oversoul. The system involved reincarnation, mystical contemplation and magic. A work of the most eclectic synthesis *The Secret Doctrine* ransacked and conjoined the Vedas, the cabbala, hermetism, alchemy and the more esoteric traditions of the West.

Yeats was well prepared to enter into Blavatsky's system of discourse having already absorbed Sinnett's *Esoteric Buddhism* and established a firm belief in the fairy lore of western Ireland. The fact that Blavatsky had been denounced as a charlatan by the Society for Psychical Research two years before does not seem to have bothered him — it had outraged his friend Charles Johnston. On the contrary it helped him to 'hammer his thoughts into unity', to apprehend a world system where the visions of Mary Battle, his uncle's clairvoyant servant, could be seen manifesting the same divine principle as the ecstasies of Boehme or the magical evocations of MacGregor Mathers.

It was probably in the following year that Yeats met MacGregor Mathers, one of the strongest influences on his entire life and thought. While working on his first collection of fairy stories, *The Celtic Twilight,* in the British Museum Library Yeats became conscious of a fellow researcher, 'a man of thirty-six or thirty-seven, in a brown velveteen coat, with a gaunt and resolute face, and an athletic body'[23] deeply absorbed in esoteric study. When he discovered that this was MacGregor Mathers, author of *The Kabbalah Unveiled* (1887), they were soon introduced and became close associates. To the end of his life Yeats, who was unusually susceptible to physical beauty and personal presence, regarded Mathers as exceptional 'in body and voice . . . so might Faust have looked in his changeless aged youth'.

Mathers was a practising magician. His book was the chief source and inspiration for the Rosicrucian society which Yeats joined in 1890, the Order of the Golden Dawn. It was in that year that the poet had been expelled from Blavatsky's theosophical society for insisting too strenuously on the practice of magic in its esoteric section. Yeats became deeply and seriously involved in the Golden Dawn, participated in its rituals and ceremonies and more dramatically in its broils and controversies. Its membership included Florence Farr, Maud Gonne, George Pollexfen, Oscar Wilde's wife Constance and Annie Horniman who was later to become patroness of the Abbey Theatre. Yeats was initiated at Fitzroy Street, on Friday 7 March 1890 and his cabbalistic name was 'Demon Est Deus Inversus' (DEDI) after his admission to the inner fifth grade of the order in 1893. His absorption in the beliefs and practices of the Golden Dawn is everywhere attested in his poems, stories and letters of these years. His commitment to its business and administration is best illustrated in a bizarre incident of 1900, ten years after his involvement in this most millenial of sodalities had begun.

In 1892 Mathers and his wife Moina, sister of Henri Bergson, moved to Paris leaving Florence Farr as head of the Order in London. Yeats remained in close communication with the couple both by letter and by frequent visits to them at their Paris flat. This friendship survived the cycle of delusion and eccentricity which afflicted MacGregor as the decade progressed. The latter intensified his altogether false [30] claim to Scots ancestry — 'MacGregor' was assumed and in time he was to drop even the 'Mathers' part of his real name — walking the boulevards in Highland dress bristling with daggers. In Yeats's account he 'remembered a title Louis XV had conferred upon a Jacobite ancestor who had fought at Pondicherry and called himself Comte de Glenstrae, and gathered about him Frenchmen and Spaniards whose titles were more shadowy.'[24] Early in 1900 MacGregor brought to a head his intermittent quarrel with the English temple by sending the notorious Aleister Crowley — 'an unspeakable mad person' in Yeats's terms — to take possession of the rooms and papers of the society. Finding the rooms unoccupied Crowley broke in and summoned the London members before him. Yeats, aided by a member named Hunter reoccupied the rooms, changed the locks and waited with a constable for Crowley's reappearance. On 19 April Crowley turned up 'wearing a black mask and in full highland costume and with a gilt dagger by his side'.[25] Crowley retreated and struck back by taking Yeats and his associates to court and losing the case. It was not the last time that Yeats was to show himself capable of swift executive action, or enlist the aid of the police. It was he who drew up the 'Statement of Recent Events' for the temple's extraordinary meeting of 21 April and presented the resolutions which put its affairs in order once again. He was now head of the Order in London. The one casualty was his friendship with Mathers who had so permeated his creative mind for those strenuous ten years.

When we speak of Yeats's 'apocalyptic' poetry we are inclined to think of later works like 'The Second Coming' and 'Meditations in Time of Civil War' which bear witness to the 'blood dimmed tide' of contemporary history — the Easter Rising, the Great War, the October Revolution, the Irish Civil War. But the sense of apocalypse is salient in his work all through the 1890s and he formally attributes the influence to Mathers.

He began to foresee changes in the world, announcing in 1893 or 1894 the imminence of immense wars. . . . Was this [31] prophecy of his, which would shortly be repeated by mediums and clairvoyants all over the world, an unconscious inference taken up into an imagination brooding upon war, or was it prevision?[26]

Either way Yeats himself in a sketch entitled 'War' published in the 1902 version of *The Celtic Twilight* describes a conversation he had with an Irish country woman: 'And presently our talk of war shifted, as it had a way of doing, to the battle of the Black Pig, which seems to her a battle between Ireland and England, but to me an Armageddon which shall quench all things in the Ancestral Darkness again. . . .' The image of that terror is to be found of course in his poem, 'The Valley of the Black Pig' with its 'clash of fallen horsemen' and the cries of 'unknown perishing armies'. It is even more prominent in the stories of *The Secret Rose* written under the emblem of the Golden Dawn, the mystical rose suffering upon the cross of time.

Published in 1897 this elaborate volume of stories traces two thousand years of Irish history – twenty centuries of stony sleep – down to the contemporary world, the *fin de siècle* — when a generation of symbolic writers is waiting for 'the trembling of the veil', the advent of the savage god. The character of Michael Robartes who dominates the world of the last three stories, 'Rosa Alchemica', 'The Tables of the Law' and 'The Adoration of the Magi' is based on Mathers, high priest of the new dispensation who died in the midst of the Great War when history was moving into that period of bloodshed which he had so feverishly prophesied.

The 1890s were in every other respect crowded and eventful in Yeats's development. His novel, *John Sherman* which was published in the same volume as the mythical tale 'Dhoya' in 1891 was a modest success with its theme of choice between London and Sligo, a concern that had occupied the Anglo-Irish novel since Edgeworth and Lady Morgan. Like

the speaker in 'The Lake Isle of Innisfree' and the eponymous
hero of the novel Yeats travelled in fact and in reverie between
the two places throughout the decade. In 1892 he brought out
his second book of poems *The Countess Cathleen and Various
Legends:* from it and its predecessor, *The Wanderings of Oisin
and Other Poems*, he was to cull the lyrics that have since made
up the volume *Crossways* in his *Collected Poems*. The following year saw the publication of his three-volume edition of
Blake in collaboration with Edwin Ellis and the appearance of
The Celtic Twilight which gave its name to the literary movement he was to inaugurate and lead. In 1894 his *Land of
Heart's Desire* served as a curtain-raiser to Shaw's *Arms and
the Man* in which Florence Farr — Shaw's mistress, head of
the Golden Dawn and probably Yeats's confidante in the
affair with Olivia Shakespear — played the part of Raina.

In that same year Yeats visited Mathers in Paris where he
saw *Axël* by Villiers de l'Isle Adam. This was an exemplary
conjunction of Rosicrucianism and symbolism, an influence
which was reinforced when he went back to Paris two years
later with Arthur Symons and saw a performance of Alfred
Jarry's *Ubu Roi*. On that visit he met Synge and probably
gave him the celebrated advice to go to the Aran Islands and
discover a life that had not yet found expression in literature.
In the same year he himself visited Aran, met Lady Gregory
at Coole and set about founding an Order of Celtic Mysteries
to be celebrated on a lake island in the west of Ireland.

Three times during the decade — in 1892, 1894 and 1899 —
he proposed marriage to Maud Gonne and was refused. The
long summer he spent in Coole Park with Lady Gregory who
probably saved him from psychic if not physical collapse. In
1899 he published his own symbolist book of poems, *The
Wind among the Reeds*, the supreme expression of 'longing and complaint — the cry of the heart against necessity'.
On 3 January 1900 Susan Yeats died of 'general paralysis' at
the Yeats home in Bedford Park, in the presence of her
husband and her eldest son who happened by chance to be
there that night. In this year the focus of the poet's energy

shifts fairly decisively to Dublin, though he continues to spend the winters at Woburn Buildings. A new adventure had [33] begun with the founding of the Irish Literary Theatre and the production of his poetic play, *The Countess Cathleen*, in 1899, at Dublin's Antient Concert Rooms.

3
'Upon the Abbey Stage'

On 8 May 1899 an English company of players including
Florence Farr and the young May Whitty, who played the
title role, performed Yeats's second play *The Countess
Cathleen* at Dublin's Antient Concert Rooms. Though Yeats
had worked hard on the script since it had been published
in 1892, fitting it for the stage in the light of his experience
with *The Land of Heart's Desire*, it was a theatrical shambles.
But as a cultural event it was outstanding, convulsing every
area of Dublin life, religious, academic and civil. Its theme
involved a saintly countess who sold her soul to demons in
order to save her people from famine. The play was condemned, unread, by Cardinal Logue, denounced by students
of the Royal University — young James Joyce was among
those refusing to sign the petition — and vigorously attacked
by a Catholic Nationalist Frank Hugh O'Donnell in a
pamphlet entitled *Souls for Gold*. On the opening night the
police were present to keep order, 'twenty men and a sergeant'
in Yeats's account. The issues of art, religion and national
culture that the play raised were debated in the pages of
Dublin's *Daily Express* by Yeats, A. E., Douglas Hyde,
Standish James O'Grady, Lady Gregory and D. P. Moran,
editor of *The Leader* and the debate was published in
volume form as *Ideals in Ireland* in 1901. It remains a
seminal document in the growth of the Irish literary
renaissance.

The actual performance is finely documented. George
Moore, who had come to settle in Dublin to partake in the
new movement, enumerated the play's disadvantages:

First, the author's theory that verse should be chanted and not spoken; second, the low platform insufficiently separated from the audience; third, a set of actors and actresses unaccustomed to speak verse; fourth, harsh, ridiculous scenery; fifth, absurd costumes. . . . Many times I prayed during the last act that the curtain might come down at once.[27]

Yeats seems to have revelled in the controversy, remarking later that it was 'a stirring row . . . and we were all very angry'. The vagaries of Irish sensibility steeled him for many future encounters.

The accusation made was that it was a libel on the people of Ireland to say that they could under any circumstances consent to sell their souls and that it was a libel on the demons that they counted the soul of a countess of more worth than those of the poor.[28]

Typically he discerned the areas where he, not the audience, had failed in tact: where an evil peasant had trampled on a Catholic shrine he blamed himself for the audience's discomfort — 'In using what I considered traditional symbols I forgot that in Ireland they are not symbols but realities.'[29]

The most significant reaction to the performance was that of Willie and Frank Fay who were later to form the backbone of the Abbey Players when that theatre was founded in 1904. They admired the acting and the verse speaking which overcame, for them, the disadvantages of the 'fit-up' stage and unsuitable hall. It took them long analysis to discover what was really lacking.

Then it suddenly flashed upon me that what was wrong with the performance was that, though the artists were most efficient, they were not Irish. To get the full value of the play one must have native actors . . . . Frank quite agreed with me, but he very pertinently asked, 'Where in Ireland could you get any company of actors that could compare with those we have just seen?'[30]

It was with that flash of insight, one could argue, that the
[36] Abbey Theatre was conceived. There would be five years
painful and exciting gestation before the final delivery at
Abbey Street in 1904.

The ideal of a literary theatre, however, had begun back in
London around 1894 when George Moore had gone to see
The Land of Heart's Desire and entered into discussions with
his cousin, Edward Martyn and Yeats about the possibility
of founding a theatre. When staying with Moore at Edward
Martyn's house, Tulira Castle in Galway, he had visited Lady
Gregory at Coole Park. The following summer he returned
to Coole Park for an extended visit and the great house with
its lake and seven woods was virtually his summer home for
the rest of his unmarried life. In that summer of 1897,
however, a momentous meeting took place at Duras House,
Co. Clare, the home of Comte de Basterot. There Yeats, Lady
Gregory and Edward Martyn determined upon the founding
of an Irish literary theatre. Their first production was Yeats's
The Countess Cathleen on 8 May 1899 which was followed
the night after by their second and most successful play,
Edward Martyn's Ibsenesque drama *The Heather Field*.
Doldrums followed. Martyn and Moore cobbled together a
piece called *The Bending of the Bough* – revised from
Martyn's *The Tale of a Town* – and presented it to mixed
critical response at the Gaiety on 20 February 1901. Then
Yeats and Moore, after a hilarious collaboration, produced a
tragedy, *Diarmuid and Grania* in October of the same year.
Both these productions were hampered by the difficulty
already outlined by Willie Fay, the Englishness of the cast.
Frank Benson's Shakespearean company records its
bewilderment with the Irish names:

they were pronouncing Diarmuid in three or four different
ways, and calling Grania 'Grawniar' or 'Grainyah'.
Matheson Lang said that, though Yeats was very particular
with pronunciation, nobody could manage the name of
Caoilte. The company called it 'Kaoltay'; Yeats said it

should be 'Wheelsher'. That night Harcourt Williams was addressed successively as 'Wheelchair', 'Coldtea', and [37] 'Quilty', to the horror of the patriots.[31]

On the same night, however, the first Irish-speaking play *Casadh an tSúgáin* by Douglas Hyde was successfully produced by Willie Fay with the author in the lead, supported by a cast of Irish actors. It was the last production by the Irish literary theatre as such, but the way forward was already clear.

On 2 April 1902 W. G. Fay's Irish National Dramatic Company produced Yeats's *Cathleen ni Houlihan* as part of a double bill with A.E.'s *Deirdre*. The play had a powerful impact on an audience already bristling with nationalist sentiment. The scenario, which came to Yeats in a 'vivid dream' concerned the French expedition of 1798 to Killala Bay to aid the Irish in the rebellion of that year. An old woman comes in off the roads to a house where a wedding is arranged. Her runic dialogue convinces the young man that he has a destiny greater than marriage. The audience becomes aware that she is no ordinary old woman but the legendary Cathleen ni Houlihan herself, Ireland incarnate, waiting for the heroic sacrifice that will give her back youth and beauty. He abandons his betrothed and rushes out to join the French. The curtain line has become fabulous:

Peter: Did you see an old woman going down the path?
Patrick: I did not, but I saw a young girl, and she had the walk of a queen.

O'Leary had already advised Yeats that he must have either the priests or the nationalists on his side. This one act play, which was to be produced over and over again, made him a temporary hero in the eyes of the patriots. More conservative opinion was distressed. The writer and statesman Stephen Gwynn wrote:

The effect of *Cathleen ni Houlihan* on me was that I went home asking myself if such plays should be produced unless one was prepared for people to go out to shoot and be

shot. Yeats was not alone responsible; no doubt but Lady
Gregory had helped him to get the peasant speech so
perfect. But above all Miss Gonne's impersonation had
stirred the audience as I have never seen another audience
stirred.[32]

In a late poem 'The Man and the Echo' Yeats was to dwell on
the play and his responsibility for it:

> I lie awake night after night
> And never get the answer right.
> Did that play of mine send out
> Certain men the English shot?

Indeed the implications of that question were to form the core
of the greatest body of poetry to confront the problem of
violence in the English language since Shakespeare.

Looking back on this period in his late poem 'The Circus
Animals' Desertion' Yeats is conscious of a strange bewilderment, of an effort to balance the pagan love quest of Oisin
against the Christian sacrifice of the Countess Cathleen, to
maintain an equilibrium between the anguish of his unrequited
love for Maud — who seemed in turn obsessed with Irish
nationalism — and the importunities of his muse:

> And then a counter-truth filled out its play,
> The *Countess Cathleen* was the name I gave it;
> She, pity-crazed, had given her soul away,
> But masterful Heaven had intervened to save it.
> I thought my dear must her own soul destroy,
> So did fanaticism and hate enslave it,
> And this brought forth a dream and soon enough
> This dream itself had all my thought and love.

On an evening in February 1903 Yeats was about to address
a public meeting in Dublin when he was handed a letter from
Maud informing him that she had just married Major John
MacBride in Paris. The afflicted poet went through with his
lecture but could never remember afterwards a word he had
said, though he received many congratulations on the quality

of his performance. This desperate hour on the podium, when
the real world so savagely intruded upon his drama of heroic [39]
love, is recalled in a poem called 'Reconciliation' written six
years later:

> Some may have blamed you that you took away
> The verses that could move them on the day
> When, the ears being deafened, the sight of the eyes blind
> With lightning, you went from me, and I could find
> Nothing to make a song about but kings,
> Helmets, and swords, and half-forgotten things
> That were like memories of you — but now
> We'll out, for the world lives as long ago;
> And while we're in our laughing, weeping fit,
> Hurl helmets, crowns, and swords into the pit.
> But, dear, cling close to me; since you were gone,
> My barren thoughts have chilled me to the bone.

His lecture tour of North America in 1903 may have helped
to distract Yeats from the emotional distress of Maud's
marriage to MacBride. The tour was organised by the New
York lawyer and bibliophile, John Quinn and took him to
several universities in the U.S. and Canada, as far west as
San Francisco and finally to a triumphant lecture at Carnegie
Hall. While in America news came to him of the successes of
the theatre in Dublin. It was a remarkable year for the fledgling
movement with Lady Gregory's first play, *Twenty Five*,
Synge's *Shadow of the Glen* and Padraic Colum's *Broken Soil*.
The national theatre had become a fact of Irish life. This news
cheered the poet as he progressed through the American con-
tinent from one success to another. John Quinn assured Lady
Gregory that he had made a greater impression on America
than anyone else since Parnell. Yeats wrote to Quinn that he
was now 'facing the world with great hopes and strength' and
the three thousand dollars he had earned by his exertions
enabled him to face his career in literature with fresh courage.

The one note of impatience sounded in the letters from
America concerns a request from his sisters for money to help

finance the Dun Emer Press back in Dublin. The Yeats family
had moved back to Dublin in 1902 where the sisters, Lily
and Lolly had joined a Miss Evelyn Gleeson in setting up the
Dun Emer Industries at Dundrum to develop Irish weaving,
embroidery, carpet making and hand printing. The poet must
have had little initial confidence in the enterprise: his letter
to Lady Gregory from San Francisco shows a natural irritation.

> I am feeling rather tired and cross – the lecturing has tired
> me a little at last and I am longing to be back and I confess
> that I do not like the thought that the first money I ever
> earned beyond the need of the moment will be expected
> to go to Dun Emer . . . and do no good there.

Dun Emer, which had published *In the Seven Woods* that July
flourished, giving birth in 1908 to the more famous Cuala
Press which was managed by the Yeats sisters until 1940 when
Lolly died. It was then taken over and managed by Yeats's
widow, George. Among the sixty-six Cuala Press titles before
its close-down in 1946 were books by A.E., Douglas Hyde,
Lady Gregory, J. M. Synge, Lord Dunsany, Rabindranath
Tagore, Ezra Pound, Louis MacNeice, Oliver Gogarty, Patrick
Kavanagh and J. B. Yeats *pere et fils*. Before he sailed from
New York on 9 March the problem at Dun Emer had subsided:
'A note from my sister. The panic has quite died out and they
say all is well.'

The year 1904 was a strenuous, tense and ultimately deci-
sive year for Yeats. His friendship with Russell was coming
under increasing strain largely because of their divergence
in mental purpose, Yeats building a life on art, Russell on
spiritual vision. Yet in his quest for hidden patterns Yeats
could find an underlying unity. Writing to Olivia Shakespear
from Coole Park in July he confided:

> I notice that whenever anybody here writes a play it always
> works out, whatever the ideas of the writer, into a cry for a
> more abundant and a more intense life. Synge and A.E. the
> poet are staying here, and though they come to their task

from the opposite side of the heavens they are both stirring the same pot — something of a witches' cauldron, I think.   [41]

Despite increasing trouble with his eyes he seemed intensely busy. In dictating a letter to Frank Fay in August he got so absorbed in his thoughts on acting and stage management that the piece becomes almost a 'poetics' of the new theatre. It seems astonishing that he had learned so fast the current theories and practices of stagecraft and so unerringly evolved an acting method suitable to his purposes. The naturalism of Antoine is as obsolescent as the fictional strategies of Zola: 'We desire an extravagant, if you will, unreal, rhetorical romantic art, allied in literature to the art on one hand of Racine and the other hand of Cervantes.'

The letter was written in order to prime Fay with arguments to use in an article against Moore's realist theories of drama. Three years earlier Yeats had been taking lessons in theatre from them both. The high romantic style was not to become the characteristic idiom of the Abbey players, but in these early years it flourished and served Yeats's heroic drama and the high comedy of Synge. Indeed the bill with which the new Abbey opened fairly epitomised the two styles of acting and writing that were to compete for the audience's favour. In December, after protracted negotiations for a patent, with a generous subsidy from Annie Horniman, the reconstructed Abbey Theatre opened its doors with Yeats's tragedy, *On Baile's Strand* and Lady Gregory's rural comedy *Spreading the News.* It was the last appearance of the Fays' Irish National Theatre Society. The Abbey Theatre, Yeats's dream of a living national theatre, had become a reality.

In 1901 Yeats had attended a sequence of Shakespeare's history plays 'with all the links that bind play to play unbroken' performed by Frank Benson's company at Stratford-on-Avon. The effect upon him had been profound, especially in the contrast he had discerned between the characters of Richard II and Henry V. He found himself bitterly opposing Dowden's moral school of criticism which condemned Richard and exalted Henry as 'Shakespeare's only hero'. This moralistic criticism Yeats called 'The Accusation of Sin' and its necessary fruit as 'hatred of all that was abundant, extravagant, exuberant, of all that sets a sail for shipwreck, and flattery of the commonplace emotions and conventional ideals of the mob, the chief Paymaster of accusation'.[33]

A powerful consistency latent in Yeats's thought from the beginning now became aggressively manifest. His stubborn refusal to see any good in George Eliot sprang from her insistence on the ethical, the prosaic values of duty and responsibility which Yeats saw at the roots of Victorian materialism and of those administrative talents that had made British imperialism prosper at the expense of smaller, more spiritual cultures throughout the world. This belief had its origins in his father's insistence on passion and imagination and was bolstered by his own mystical and magical pursuits of the 1890s. It received a powerful impulse from his immersion in Blake whose work he had already edited with Edwin Ellis in 1893. We find it entering his lyric poetry as a combative force – as distinct from 'longing' and 'complaint' – around 1903, when he dismisses in 'Adam's Curse' the 'noisy set / Of bankers, schoolmasters, and clergymen / The martyrs call the world.'

The obvious counterpoise to the ethical materialism of 'this noisy set' is the poet – in Yeats's visionary concept of a poet – and the poet's alter ego, the hero. Two years before the production of *On Baile's Strand* Yeats had begun to read Nietzsche. The heroic figure of Cuchulain who confronts the administrative guile of the High King has in Yeats's thought an elaborate genesis. Its other versions in the plays of these years are the poet Seanchan opposing the King and the Mayor in *The King's Threshold*, Naoise and Deirdre downfacing Conchubar in *Deirdre* and Cuchulain defying death in *The Green Helmet* (1910) which ends with the assertion:

> And I choose the laughing lip
> That shall not turn from laughing, whatever rise or fall;

The heart that grows no bitterer although betrayed by all;
The hand that loves to scatter; the life like a gambler's throw;   [43]
And I these things make prosper, till a day come that I know,
When heart and mind shall darken that the weak may end
                                                    the strong,
And the long-remembering harpers have matter for their
                                                    song.

The values celebrated here are what Nietzsche had characterised as 'Dionysian' as opposed to the 'Apollonian' values of
reason and social harmony. Eventually Yeats was to construct
his theory of history and of human personality on the opposition between the 'antithetical' and the 'primary' impulses of
the psyche, terms which accord respectively with the forces
of Dionysus and Apollo in Nietzsche's *Birth of Tragedy*.

We therefore understand why Yeats has written to Frank
Fay urging a romantic, extravagant style of acting and why he
opposes, successfully, Moore's attempts to promote the
naturalism of Antoine. The production of *On Baile's Strand*
seemed to justify him. It enchanted his father who was as much
taken by the high passion of the hero's tragic predicament as
for the father /son conflict that forms the play's central action:

I cannot tell you how much I enjoyed your play. As I lay
awake most of the night I had plenty of time to think
about it. The scene between father and son over the duel
was the most thrilling and enthralling experience I ever
went through. You touched at the same moment the
fountain of joy and tears.[34]

But though the father approved the cult of the hero in the
plays he distrusted its appearance in his son's life and character. The poet had begun to revel in what he termed 'theatre
business, management of men'. In 1905 he set on foot moves
for 'the end of the democracy' at the Abbey and to have Lady
Gregory, Synge and himself set up as its Directors.

In January 1906, the year in which this directorate came
into being, he wrote to Russell in a tone that cannot have

improved an already strained relationship.

[44]

> I desire the love of a very few people, my equals or my superiors. The love of the rest would be a bond and an intrusion. These others will in time come to know that I am a fairly strong and capable man and that I have gathered the strong and capable about me, and all who love work better than idle talk will support me. It is a long fight but that is the sport of it. The antagonism, which is sometimes between you and me, comes from the fact that though you are strong and capable yourself you gather the weak and not very capable about you.

In the same letter he expresses 'no objection to a rival theatre' and the fate of the few rival movements that did begin seems to confirm Yeats's belief that the rule of the few rather than the many was the better way forward.

The theatre's success was striking. In 1905 Lady Gregory showed another side of her talent with two historical dramas, *Kincora* and *The White Cockade*; Padraic Colum proved his staying power with a new peasant drama, *The Land* and the most popular comic playwright of the decade William Boyle wrote *The Building Fund* which he followed with *The Eloquent Dempsey* in January of the following year. Yeats's heroic tragedy *Deirdre* appeared at the end of that season while they had in rehearsal a comedy which would once again put his Nietzschean strength and pugnacity to the test against the multitude. He was on tour in Scotland when the curtain rose on Synge's *Playboy of the Western World* but news of the first night riots — via Lady Gregory's telegram 'Audience broke up at use of the word shift' — brought him quickly back to Dublin. Since *The Countess Cathleen* itself, a number of events had been building up for a confrontation between Yeats and the Dublin public and the poet was positively eager to take them on.

The Shadow of the Glen with its picture of a loveless marriage and an unfaithful wife had been taken by Arthur Griffith and his Sinn Féin adherents as a libel on rural Catholic Ireland.

It had been the occasion of Dudley Digges and Maire Quinn resigning from the company. Then Padraic Colum's anti- recruiting play, *The Saxon Shilling*, had been rejected to the anger of the nationalists inside and outside the theatre. *The Well of the Saints* with its puzzling treatment of religion, superstition and miracle had done little to reassure the audiences as to the intentions of three Anglo-Irish Protestant director-playwrights in charge of a national theatre which seemed increasingly insensitive to the people's self-image. These sensibilities were waiting to be affronted when the curtain went up on *The Playboy of the Western World* on Saturday 22 January 1907. In the court case that followed the riots it was made quite clear that the uproar which greeted the opening exchanges had been deliberately orchestrated. But the shades of the Antient Concert Rooms arose when at the end of the first act the police arrived and lined the auditorium. To the credit of the players, many of whom did not like the play, they continued through the week despite being almost totally unheard. Their patience was especially tried when Robert Gregory brought in some of his Trinity friends to give moral support to the actors. High farce developed as the students broke into 'God Save the King' — whether through mischief or tactlessness — leaving the embattled players with the worst of both worlds.

When Yeats returned to Dublin he showed his judgment in rejecting every suggestion that the play should be taken off: Synge was the one great playwright of the movement and the *Playboy* was his masterpiece. He also showed his courage and political nerve by calling an open debate in the theatre. The most stirring account of that turbulent occasion is given by Mary Colum, later wife of the playwright, who was present with a group of her friends from University College Dublin, evidence that all students of the new university had not joined in the agitation against immoral literature.

A motley mixture of workmen, students, and bourgeoisie in evening dress filled the theatre, most of them with denunciatory speeches ready to deliver. Yeats took the platform in full evening dress and faced the crowd. Step by step he interpreted the play, delivering in the process some of his most complex theories of art, one moment cowing the audience, the next shouted down by them. . . . Even on the patriotics Yeats was equal to them. 'The author of *Cathleen ni Houlihan* addresses you,' he said. The audience, remembering that passionately patriotic play, forgot its antagonism for a few moments and Yeats got his cheers. . . . I never witnessed a human being fight as Yeats fought that night, nor knew another with so many weapons in his armory.[35]

His father, now living in Dublin, was Yeats's sole support from the stage and the old man's gift of oratory seems to have been equal to the occasion, if we are to judge by a late poem in which the son recalls the event:

> My father upon the Abbey stage, before him a raging crowd:
> 'This Land of Saints,' and then as the applause died out,
> 'Of plaster Saints'; his beautiful mischievous head thrown
> back.

It was a famous victory for Yeats. Though he suffered unpopularity at home he had the satisfaction of seeing the *Playboy* acclaimed in London before the year was out. His letter to Quinn on the subject contains a typically trenchant analysis of play and audience: 'They never minded Boyle, whose people are a sordid lot, because they knew what he was at . . . but they shrink from Synge's harsh, independent, heroic, clean, wind-swept view of things.' Yeats overlooks, however, the fact that Boyle was one of them, not an Ascendency Protestant looking in upon them from without. As a matter of record William Boyle withdrew his plays in protest against the *Playboy*, returning them in 1912, three years after the death of Synge. For the moment Yeats had both the priests and the nationalists against him and he was totally unrepentant.

The self-confidence with which Yeats confronted and

downfaced the Abbey audience had been hard bought, arduously developed by his debates in the Contemporary Club, the *Cheshire Cheese* and the meetings of countless literary societies in Ireland and England. It was compounded of passion and reserve, hauteur and persuasiveness and ultimately, with the signs auspicious, a determination to take on the enemy in the open field. The enemy, as we have seen, is the middle class with its conventional morals, social respectabilities and distrust of the unusual, the extravagant; what Yeats was later to call the 'wasteful virtues'. He had opposed to these values those of poet, visionary, magician and hero. These concepts are now joined and, as it were, crowned by the ideal of the aristocrat.

His great love poem 'Adam's Curse' had already shown the influence of Castiglione's *Book of the Courtier* which Yeats was reading in Hoby's translation at the turn of the century. Now in April 1907 Yeats went on a tour of the Renaissance cities of Northern Italy, visiting Florence, Milan, Ferrara, Ravenna and above all Urbino, the setting for Castiglione's great treatise on the courtly ideal. Yeats was deeply and permanently impressed by the achievements of the Renaissance princes in their patronage of painting, sculpture, architecture and poetry. Thereafter 'Urbino's windy hill' became an ideal society, an example of what he called 'unity of being', where patron, priest, artist and artisan formed a community fused and harmonised by a vision of human excellence. It is as if the world of Castiglione had endorsed the stance Yeats had taken for the arts against the market-place on the Abbey stage a month before in Dublin. From then on he was confirmed in a position from which he could challenge the 'levelling spirit' whether it called itself communism, socialism, whiggery, egalitarianism, humanitarianism or democracy itself.

The career of the poet's father, John Butler Yeats, had taken a new turn in October 1901 when his offerings had all been turned down by the judges of the Royal Hibernian Academy. The dynamic and business-like Sarah Purser had decided to strike back on his behalf and that of Nathaniel

Hone, another distinguished painter who had been treated [48] with undeserved neglect by the Academy. Sarah Purser put on an exhibition of the two men's work at the Royal Society of Antiquaries on Stephen's Green. It had considerable success and though it brought the impoverished sixty-two-year-old painter few financial rewards it helped him by attracting the attention of John Quinn in New York. Few Irish writers or artists of that period managed to avoid Quinn's discriminating benevolence. The Yeats family was still in London and when Quinn went there on a visit from New York in 1902 he met the sisters and Jack B. Yeats and bought a dozen of the young man's paintings. In Dublin he met all of the Irish *literati* and began an association with the father that lasted till the old man's death.

John B. Yeats was now a celebrated figure in the Dublin artistic world with the weight and eloquence to bear a pioneer role in the imminent controversy over the Lane pictures. It was John B. Yeats who first challenged the Royal Hibernian Academy on the issue of finding a suitable gallery to house Sir Hugh Lane's collections of modern pictures and raising funds to buy others. The arrival of his daughters to set up the Dun Emer project in 1902 led to their settling in Dublin, at Gurteen Dhas, from which the combative old man sallied out to fight for art and theatre, to enthrall Dublin society as a dinner guest and to undertake if not immediately execute portraits of his contemporaries. It was as a reasonably distinguished public man that the elder Yeats accepted an invitation from Quinn to visit America in 1907. That was the year in which his son, Willie, returned from Italy to do battle with the philistines on the Lane pictures issue. Fourteen years later John B. Yeats was still in New York when he died in 1922.

Sir Hugh Lane, nephew of Lady Gregory was an inspired picture dealer and conceived a plan for a gallery of modern art for Dublin City. In 1904 he exhibited three collections: one was a private collection of impressionist paintings which he hoped to donate to the proposed municipal gallery; the other two he hoped would be bought out of a fund raised out of contributions from the Corporation and private donations. The Royal Hibernian Academy led by its President, Sir Thomas Drew (John B. Yeats's old enemy) opposed the plan. But a vigorous campaign mounted by the Yeatses and their friends persuaded a great number of private donors and the Corporation to give it their support. The project would almost certainly have succeeded if Lane had not insisted on a gallery to be built over the Halfpenny Bridge on the River Liffey and designed by Sir Edwin Luytens, an Englishman. The dispute lasted until Lane's death aboard the *Lusitania* on its voyage from New York in 1915. The rights and wrongs of the case are hard to unravel, but those who read Yeats's suite of poems on the subject can be forgiven for blaming everyone except the far from blameless Lane himself. But his insistence on a Dublin Ponte Vecchio was ill-advised and his insistence on his own choice of architect a little provocative. The Corporation actually agreed to vote £22,000 in 1913 towards a building, and private donations in Ireland, England and America had been generous. Satiric poetry cannot be expected, however to agonise over such nuances of controversy.

The situation was a godsend for a poet who had just returned from a country where patronage of the arts exhibited the true aristocratic spirit, and to a poet who was reshaping his style as a more muscular, combative instrument to encounter the realities of the new century. His poem, 'Upon a House Shaken by the Land Agitation' in his collection *The Green Helmet* (1910) may be seen as his first major profession of aristocratic faith. In a draft note to the poem he explains that Coole Park 'has enriched my soul out of measure because life moves here without restraint through gracious forms ... no compelled labour, no poverty-thwarted impulse.' The poem laments that the estate must be diminished, because of the recent land acts, to increase the holdings of its tenant farmers.

How should the world be luckier if this house,
Where passion and precision have been one
Time out of mind, became too ruinous

To breed the lidless eye that loves the sun?
[50] And the sweet laughing eagle thoughts that grow
Where wings have memory of wings, and all
That comes of the best knit to the best?

So far it is celebratory, elegiac, the first of many great poems
devoted to Coole Park and the values that it fostered. But it
goes on with a startling objection to social change and a
strange slur on that peasantry who had figured so finely in his
previous poems and stories:

Although
Mean roof trees were the sturdier for its fall,
How should their luck run high enough to reach
The gifts that govern men, and after these
To gradual Time's last gift, a written speech
Wrought of high laughter, loveliness and ease?

Clearly the peasantry are to be commended once they stay
poor and mystical, not when they grow sturdier and aspire to
the middle classes. But however *high* they go they cannot
rise to the condition of a Gregory or a Yeats? The levelling
spirit is downwards. This is to be a major theme in Yeats, too
complex to explore in all its implications here. But the stance
is unequivocal and he states it to a world where agrarian
reform, militant nationalism and the Labour movement of
Connolly and Larkin make up the context of his days, sometimes supplying him with his best allies.

His next volume *Responsibilities* (1914) gathers into it
much of the fervour and bitterness that enlivened these
turbulent years. Maud Gonne's marriage had long broken
up and he visited her regularly at her house in Normandy
where she lived with her children, Seán and Iseult. On one of
her rare visits to Dublin he had taken her to the Abbey where
she had been hissed by the nationalist adherents of MacBride.
Yeats had accepted a civil list pension of £150 – on condition
that he could go on writing as he wished on Irish politics –
and had been attacked in the nationalist press as a 'pensioner'

of the British. The personal abuse poured upon the 'picture-dealer' Lane had hurt far more than the frustration and defeat of the plan for a gallery. In 1913 Jim Larkin, an ally of Yeats and Lane in the dispute, led the Dublin workers in a massive strike against the Dublin employers led by William Martin Murphy, transport magnate and founder of the *Irish Independent*. Though no enthusiast for socialism Yeats could not resist taking the side of the workers in the papers and on the platforms and drawing on himself increased abuse and odium. In the background there was the sardonic chuckle of his former friend, George Moore, whose trilogy, *Hail and Farewell* had come out 1911–1914 with Yeats as its chief object of mockery. Moore's derision — witty and vivid in hindsight — was especially galling in its scorn for Yeats's pretensions to aristocracy.

No wonder therefore that *Responsibilities* is a fighting book. Yeats opens defiantly with a celebration of his ancestors, those 'old fathers' whose blood has not passed 'through any huckster's loin':

A Butler or an Armstrong that withstood
Beside the brackish waters of the Boyne
James and his Irish when the Dutchman crossed;

In the poems that follow the huckster is counterpoised against the aristocrat. The Yeats ancestors whether 'trading out of Galway into Spain' or out of Sligo into Liverpool were merchants but not hucksters. Their passion and generosity, their cultivation of the 'wasteful virtues', made them aristocrats. Paudeen and Biddy fumbling in their greasy Dublin till were hucksters. Less obvious a huckster was Lord Ardilaun in 'To a Wealthy Man who promised a Second Subscription to the Dublin Municipal Gallery if it were proved the People wanted Pictures'. When the piece appeared in *The Irish Times* on 11 January 1913, Murphy thought he was the wealthy man in question – which means that he must have subscribed in the first place – so he redoubled his invective against Yeats. It did not strike him that the scion of Guinness could be defined as a huckster by the son of a penniless portrait painter. He

was not the last to mistake Yeats's subtle and elaborate
[52] concept of the aristocratic:

> You gave, but will not give again
> Until enough of Paudeen's pence
> By Biddy's halfpennies have lain
> To be 'some sort of evidence',
> Before you'll put your guineas down,
> That things it were a pride to give
> Are what the blind and ignorant town
> Imagines best to make it thrive.

Not pausing to note how many factions he had antagonised
in this opening Yeats sweeps into his litany of real aristocratic
patrons: Duke Ercole who had commissioned the comedies
of Plautus to be played for his daughter's wedding, Cosimo
the Great who had built the San Marco Library, and most
importantly

> . . . Guidobaldo, when he made
> That grammar school of courtesies
> Where wit and beauty learned their trade
> Upon Urbino's windy hill,
> Had sent no runners to and fro
> That he might learn the shepherds' will.

The exhortation ends with a return to the eagle image of
'Upon a House' — the royal bird that alone can look into
the sun:

> Look up in the sun's eye and give
> What the exultant heart calls good
> That some new day may breed the best
> Because you gave, not what they would,
> But the right twigs for an eagle's nest.

In 'September 1913' the ghost of John O'Leary is invoked
to rebuke an unredeemed political scene where 'men were
born to pray and save' in a world of damp materialism
uncannily reminiscent — as the whole volume is — of the city

conjured up by Joyce's *Dubliners*. The shade of Parnell who presides so desolately over Joyce's committee room is the [53] accusing ghost of a poem that follows 'To a Shade'. Hugh Lane is compared to him in the poem's second bitter movement.

> A man of your own passionate serving kind who had brought
> In his full hands what, had they only known,
> Had given their children's children loftier thought,
> Sweeter emotion, working in their veins
> Like gentle blood, has been driven from the place,
> And insult heaped upon him for his pains,
> And for his open-handedness, disgrace;
> Your enemy, an old foul mouth, had set
> The pack upon him.

Murphy, whose 'Bantry gang' led by Tim Healy was credited with the defeat of Parnell, is the 'old foul mouth' in question. The imagery of the noble stag pulled down by hounds, used also by Joyce, is to recur in Yeats's relentless dialogue with contemporary history. Lane earns his title to nobility by 'serving' as his aunt had served. Art is not just decorative or even merely beautiful, its contemplation refines the blood of generations, 'gentles our condition'. Yeats is vehement because he is playing for high cultural stakes.

Responsibilities points some further emphases in the poet's life and work. The death of Synge in 1909 was an irreparable loss and marked the end of the Abbey's first great phase: 'the best labourer dead / and all the sheaves to bind'. His meeting with Ezra Pound in 1912 had a far-reaching effect on his poetic practice. Pound married Olivia Shakespear's daughter and Yeats returned from an American visit to attend the wedding in 1914. His stay with Pound at Stone Cottage in Sussex in the autumn of 1913 cemented a friendship of great creativity which lasted for more than a decade. Pound taught Yeats how to fence; Yeats inducted Pound into the mysteries of spiritualism. Pound was then editing Ernest Fenollosa's Japanese Noh plays from which Yeats found the means to a

new development in his drama. Yeats wrote 'The Witch' and
[54] 'The Peacock' and Pound immortalised the occasion in the
Cantos:

> so that I recalled the noise in the chimney
> as it were the wind in the chimney
>> but was in reality Uncle William
> downstairs composing
> that had made a great Peeeeacock
>> in the proide ov his oiye

But *Responsibilities* ends bitterly with a 'closing rhyme' which
he had thought of entitling 'Notoriety'. A sort of coda to the
hard years of controversy it presents the poet withdrawing,
like a Ben Jonson or an Andrew Marvell, to the sanctuary
of Coole to recover from the abuse and slander of the market-
place

> *when June is come*
> *At Kyle-na-no under that ancient roof*
> *A sterner conscience and a friendlier home,*
> *I can forgive even the wrong of wrongs,*
> *Those undreamt accidents that have made me*
> *– Seeing that Fame has perished this long while,*
> *Being but a part of ancient ceremony –*
> *Notorious, till all my priceless things*
> *Are but a post that passing dogs defile.*

4

'All Changed, Changed Utterly'

One might easily have expected that Yeats had finished with Irish themes and symbols on the publication of *Responsibilities*. The production of *The Green Helmet* (1910), his 'heroic farce' on the Cuchulain theme to all intents and purposes ended for at least ten years his involvement as a playwright in the Abbey theatre workshop. The penultimate poem in *Responsibilities*, 'A Coat', seemed a formal shuffling off of Gaelic legend:

I made my song a coat
Covered with embroideries
Out of old mythologies
From heel to throat;
But the fools caught it,
Wore it in the world's eyes
As though they'd wrought it.
Song, let them take it.
For there's more enterprise
In walking naked.

But he was resilient. The roots of his patriotism were as deep as those of his love for Maud and beneath the surface they were curiously intertwined. He had not given up hope of marrying her, nor had she yet cancelled all hope of his acceptance. His visits to Normandy were further enhanced by his deepening friendship with Iseult, his 'child dancing in the wind'. Back in Dublin in 1915 he cannot resist the temptation of sharing a platform in a Thomas Davis commemoration ceremony with Patrick Pearse and Thomas Kettle who was shortly to lose his life in the Great War. The fact that Mahaffy

had refused to allow 'a man called Pearse' inside Trinity's gate for the meeting proved an irresistible incentive to the poet. But the mobility and interest of his life was perhaps the major cause of his strength and buoyancy. In Coole, Dublin, London, New York and Paris he had to hand 'a scene well set and excellent company'. During the winter months his flat at Woburn Buildings was the scene of a literary gathering every Monday evening. London hostesses were at turns charmed, intrigued, intimidated and wearied by his strange presence, elegant, fey and formidable.

Cuchulain was reborn for him in London 1916 when the Abbey players performed *On Baile's Strand* in costumes specially designed by Charles Ricketts. He wrote exultantly to Quinn: 'I am full of new poems – dramatic and lyrical. All my mythological people have come alive again and I want to complete my heroic cycle.' He spent the winter at Stone Cottage with the newly-married Pounds and early in 1916 dictated to Ezra that splendid product of their propinquity *At the Hawk's Well*, a Noh play on the Cuchulain theme. The play marks Yeats's break with the conventional theatre of his day. To achieve the ritual intimacy of his drama he needed a small theatre and a select audience which could be relied on to attend to every nuance of dance, speech and music. The first performance was in Lady Cunard's drawing-room at Cavendish Square on the afternoon of Sunday 2 April 1916. Only invited guests were admitted and the press was firmly excluded. The costumes and masks were designed by Edmond Dulac and a Japanese dancer, Michio Ito, played the part of the guardian of the well. The performance gave Yeats enormous satisfaction making him 'happier than Sophocles . . . as lucky as a Japanese dramatic poet at the Court of the Shogun'.[36] Far from being a passing luxury this sort of coterie theatre remained Yeats's ideal for the rest of his creative life. He continued to be the shrewdest reader at the Abbey Theatre when it came to judging the viability of a realist play. But the thrust of his own genius was for the total theatre of dance, song, music, speech, ritual, gesture, a form of theatre that has only come into its own in recent decades. In his last play, *The Death of Cuchulain* (1939), he has a prologue in which he wishes for an audience of friends, no more in number 'than those who listened to the first performance of *Comus*'. But by then he had by this exclusive medium produced such a universal masterpiece as *Purgatory* – one of the great seminal works of the modern theatre.

When Yeats was working towards his concept of an exclusive theatre James Joyce, who had warned him so sharply against the lure of the 'rabblement' fifteen years before, was being forced out of Trieste with his family to Zurich by the war. Yeats, with customary generosity, beat the bushes in London to get him financial assistance from the Royal Literary Fund, managing at the end of the day a subvention of £75. Two years before he had received an unexpected fee of £50 from *Poetry* in Chicago and had gone to remarkable lengths to have it directed towards the needier Ezra Pound. But as Joyce dodged the Great War round Europe and Yeats recast in ritual the heroic wars of Cuchulain in Cavendish Square, revolutionary war broke out in Dublin in Easter Week 1916. Yeats was staying with William Rothenstein, the painter, in Gloucestershire, when the word reached him and it is reported that he 'fretted somewhat that he had not been consulted, had been left in ignorance of what was afoot'.

His letter to Lady Gregory of 11 May is already eloquent with the sense of tragedy that permeates his poem 'Easter 1916' which he seems to have begun. He quotes Maud Gonne's pronouncement 'tragic dignity has returned to Ireland'. The refrain of his poem is already forming in his mind – 'terrible beauty has been born again'. To Quinn he writes that Ireland has lost 'the ablest and most fine-natured of our young men'. He wonders whether he 'could have done anything to turn those young men in some other direction'. The question is to take a sharper form before he dies: 'Did that play of mine send out / Certain men the English shot?' But there is almost a sense of pre-determination about his second paragraph.

At the moment I feel as I shall return to Dublin to live, to begin building again. I look sadly about my rooms for I have just taken in and furnished the floor below my old rooms and so have practically the whole house. I am pleased with the look of things and shall be sad to shift. Yet perhaps tomorrow I may be in another mood and not sad at the thought or have given the thought up. I chiefly dread the temptation of controversy one finds in Dublin. I knew several of the executed men, and others were familiar figures. . . .

He did not give up the thought. Twice that year he visited the devastated city. On his return from the June visit he wrote to Robert Bridges that all his 'habits of thought and work are upset by this tragic Irish rebellion which has swept away friends and fellow workers'. He was, in the meantime, trying to get a passport to visit 'a friend in Normandy who has been greatly troubled by it all'. During his visit to Maud he wrote the poem. He proposed to her again now that she was free; her husband died in the executions that followed the Rising. She declined again and with her permission he proposed to her daughter Iseult who also turned him down but with no great finality.

His second visit to Dublin, towards the end of 1916, was full of business. He set about buying the tower at Ballylee which was to give its name to his greatest single volume of poetry. He bought it for £35 from the Congested Districts Board together with a cottage at its base and set in train plans to have it re-roofed and renovated to serve as a summer home. Writing to Olivia Shakespear he seemed 'very busy, reading plays, seeing plays at the Abbey, seeing numerous people about business'. The Lane pictures controversy was raging anew as Britain had refused to recognise the signed but unwitnessed codicil which Lane had made to his will, before embarking for America, leaving the pictures to Ireland. Yeats's letters to *The Observer* on the subject, culminating with his great summary letter of 21 January 1917, are striking evidence of his tenacity, eloquence and skill in argument.

In July of 1917 he was back in Dublin seeing to the repairs on the tower and revelling in Dublin's literary society. He stayed with Oliver Gogarty, 'the witty doctor' and had a good bust done of himself in bronze by Albert Power. 'Stephens and Russell and Hyde all called to see me and some less known people and I lived in a whirl of excellent talk. I am glad to be out of London where I am disconsolate and mostly tired.' In August he was back in Normandy, this time angling determinedly for Iseult, braving the weird menagerie with which Maud constantly surrounded herself: 'the usual number of cage birds, a parrot, a monkey, a goat, two dogs, a cat and seven rabbits'. Iseult unfortunately was moody and unwell while her mother was in 'a joyous and self-forgetting condition of political hate the like of which I have not yet encountered'. But again she turned him down, though not without vacillation and remorse.

The three returned to London in early September and encountered such difficulties with the authorities that it became impossible for them to proceed to Ireland. Difficulty in getting back to France forced Iseult to stay in London. Maud was having trouble with the Defence of the Realm Act. Writing to Lady Gregory Yeats begged for 'a letter of counsel' as Maud 'will certainly do something wild' while Iseult needs his 'friendship and [to] watch over her interests in the next few weeks'. Meanwhile he had an invitation from a certain Mrs Tucker, married to a brother of Olivia Shakespear, who lived with her daughter of a previous marriage, Georgiana Hyde-Lees, whom Yeats had already noticed and liked in Woburn Buildings. Next day, in one of those leaps of resolution that so often characterise his actions, he wrote again: 'I am going to Mrs Tucker's in the country on Saturday or Monday at the latest and I will ask her daughter to marry me. . . . I shall however make it clear that I will still be friend and guardian to Iseult'. With Ezra Pound as his best man he married George Hyde-Lees on 20 October 1917. In the early days of the marriage he felt

remorse and guilt at having 'betrayed three people'. But
[60] George who seems to have known a great deal of his mind
(they had attended seances together in London) took a piece
of paper and wrote in seemingly automatic script 'with the
bird [Iseult] all is well at heart. Your action was right for
both but in London you mistook its meaning.' This sign
from the ether was clearly the one best calculated to calm
the guilty poet. George's capacity for automatic writing was
to be a cementing force in their marriage and a continuing
source of inspiration for his work in the years ahead.

Before the end of the year she had moved into Woburn
Buildings with him and transformed, without disturbing, his
bachelor residence. Writing to Lady Gregory — whose approval
was vital to his peace of mind — he said with his characteristic
blend of tenderness and skill: 'My wife is a perfect wife, kind,
wise and unselfish. I think you were such a young girl once.
She has made my life serene and full of order. I wish you
should see Woburn Buildings now — nothing changed in plan
but little touches here and there. . . .' And what better guar-
antee of a warm welcome at Coole for the young bride than
the final sentence: 'George is reading your *Gods and Fighting
Men* and is about half way through. She prefers it to the Eddas
which she had been reading just before.'

Yeats's excited response to the Easter Rising quickly trans-
lated itself into literature: his second Noh play *The Dreaming
of the Bones* and a suite of lyrics of which 'Easter 1916' is
the most famous. He completed the play while staying with
Maude Gonne in France in 1917. Writing to Lady Gregory
he felt that it was 'I am afraid only too powerful politically'.
The theme and setting are finely adapted to the conventions
of the Noh and to Yeats's evolving thought about the spirits
of the dead. A young soldier who had fought with the rebels
in the General Post Office comes upon the ghosts of two
lovers who are locked in a perpetual dance of pain for a crime
committed while alive. It is revealed that they are the spirits of
Diarmuid and Dervorgilla who in the twelfth century had
betrayed Ireland to the Normans and that they will never be

released from their agony until 'somebody of their race at last would say, "I have forgiven them"'. In the play's implac- able ending the young man not only refuses his aid but repeats that 'never, never, / Shall Diarmuid and Dervorgilla be forgiven.' The ending derives in part from the poet's frank detestation of Britain's history in Ireland and in part, perhaps, from the mood in which the Abbey curtain had fallen on Lady Gregory's *Dervorgilla* exactly ten years before.

> My curse upon all that brought in the Gall,
> Upon Diarmuid's call, and on Dervorgilla!

But despite the power of its political feeling *The Dreaming of the Bones* is not a propagandist play. Trapped within the Noh ritual, it lacks the kinetic impulse of *Cathleen ni Houlihan*. And despite the upbeat of its famous refrain 'Easter 1916' can be read only by the simple-minded as a celebration or endorsement of armed nationalism. The fervour for 'all that blood' of September 1913 has been tempered by the senseless slaughter of the Great War and his fear that the Rising may have overturned for Yeats himself 'all the works of years, all the bringing together of classes, all the freeing of Irish literature and criticism from politics'.[37] The tension between these feelings of regret and compunction, and his natural desire to salute a living version of the heroism that his plays had celebrated through Cuchulain, gives the poem that splendid poise between pathos and irony that ensures its greatness.

Using the dramatic method perfected in 'Adam's Curse' Yeats places himself back in Dublin before the Rising so that the 'polite meaningless words', the mocking tale or jibe that he had uttered at the expense of the revolutionaries recoil in accusation on himself. Thus he takes upon himself something of the spite of the 'unmannerly town' together with its blindness to the possibilities of heroism and sacrifice that were stirring there. For a moment at least there is a fusion of identity between poet and citizenry, equal partners in the 'casual comedy' of unredeemed existence.

Being certain that they and I
But lived where motley is worn:
All changed, changed utterly:
A terrible beauty is born.

The second stanza returns to that fallen version of individual
life: the Countess's 'ignorant good will', Pearse who had 'kept
a school', MacDonagh who might have been exceptional,
MacBride, the 'drunken, vainglorious lout'. The tragic action
has transformed them all: life has become drama, poetic
imagination has for the moment worked its transfiguring
power over life's least promising matter.

It is here, after the second refrain, that the poem turns.
Transformations go on: human hearts are 'enchanted to a
stone', Cathleen ni Houlihan, Medusa-like, can make 'a stone
of the heart' and the process may never end — 'O when may
it suffice?' Thus when the poem's heroic crescendo has been
reached in its close the mood of celebration has been severely
challenged by both pity and irony.

We know their dream; enough
To know they dreamed and are dead;
And what if excess of love
Bewildered them till they died?
I write it out in a verse —
MacDonagh and MacBride
And Connolly and Pearse
Now and in time to be,
Wherever green is worn,
Are changed, changed utterly:
A terrible beauty is born.

What is most remarkable about the poem and its companions —
'Sixteen Dead Men', 'The Rose Tree' and 'On a Political
Prisoner' — is the speed with which Yeats fastened upon the
mythic nature of the Rising: Pearse's doctrine of the blood
sacrifice that had been shared by MacDonagh and others.
'The Rose Tree' links the notion of redemptive bloodshed

with the political rose of De Vere, Mangan and his own early poetry. 'Sixteen Dead Men' enthrones the patriots in a company they had been contemptuously denied in 'September 1913' – 'Lord Edward and Wolfe Tone'. Yet the imagery is distancing: the 'boiling pot' of political discontent, the 'red blood', 'MacDonagh's bony thumb'. Also his incorrigible sense of class – abetted by his Lear-like aversion to shrillness in women – impels him to see Constance Markievicz's involvement in the struggle as a defilement whereas for the others it had been an ennoblement:

> Her thought a popular enmity:
> Blind and leader of the blind
> Drinking the foul ditch where they lie?

Despite these intrinsic reservations about insurrection, the political climate prevented Yeats from publishing the poems until November 1920 when they appeared in *The Dial* prior to their inclusion in his next volume but one, *Michael Robartes and the Dancer* (1921). By then the Great War had claimed his 'dear friend's dear son' Major Robert Gregory, who had been shot down over Italy on 23 January 1918. Yeats devoted four poems to his memory. One of them, 'Reprisals', is so bitter that he refrained from publishing it in his lifetime lest it give offence to Gregory's widow. Its anger is directed against the Black and Tans, the undisciplined paramilitary force sent over by Britain to put down the Irish rebels who had taken the national struggle into a new phase of guerilla warfare. Yeats and his wife and baby daughter, Anne, have moved into their castle home, Thoor Ballylee as the Tans begin their rampage through the neighbourhood, shooting among others a nursing mother at her doorway in Gort. He calls upon Gregory to rise 'from his Italian tomb' and go to Kiltartan to see what shame has come upon 'the cause you served'.

> Half-drunk or whole-mad soldiery
> Are murdering your tenants there.
> Men that revere your father yet

Are shot at in the open plain.

Where may new-married women sit
And suckle children now? Armed men
May murder them in passing by
Nor law nor parliament take heed.
Then close your ears with dust and lie
Among the other cheated dead.

In the war poems of this period it is clear that the beauty of
1916 has now given way to the ugly and impersonal terror
of war. The horizon of his vision widens to take in the Russian
Revolution of 1917. The armed chaos that it brought in its
wake throughout eastern Europe seemed to confirm him in a
belief that the apocalypse of which he and Mathers had spoken
in the 1890s was now impending. In 'The Second Coming'

Things fall apart; the centre cannot hold;
Mere anarchy is loosed upon the world,
The blood-dimmed tide is loosed, and everywhere
The ceremony of innocence is drowned;
The best lack all conviction, while the worst
Are full of passionate intensity.

The poem culminates in an image of the coming chaos and
terror with the ending of the Christian millenia, the 'twenty
centuries of stony sleep' as the 'rough beast' of the new dispensation 'Slouches towards Bethlehem to be born'. In a letter
to Ethel Mannin sixteen years later and against a background
of political barbarism throughout Europe Yeats looked back
at this poem and claimed it as prophecy – 'it foretold what
is happening. I have written the same thing again and again
since.' And a feature of his apocalyptic poems through the
next decade is the moral terrorism of their imagery: rough
beasts, brazen hawks, 'Herodias's daughters' riding on the
wind, unicorns, swans, witches and incubi presaging the over-
throw of order and innocence as the old structures collapse
before the new terror.

5
'This Stormbeaten Place'

The visit to Lady Gregory promised for early 1918 was post-poned due to Yeats's influenza and rumours of unrest in the Galway area. It was further postponed by the news of Robert Gregory's death. As the Yeatses had let their house in Woburn Buildings they determined upon a temporary residence at Oxford until conditions in Ireland were suitable for George's first visit to the country. By January they had settled into a pleasant house at 45 Broad Street. George immediately entered into correspondence with Raftery the builder who was to restore the tower and more momentously with her Instructors, the source of her automatic writing. In a letter of 7 January Yeats wrote to Lady Gregory of a 'very profound, very exciting mystical philosophy – the fulfil-ment of many dreams and prophecies . . . coming in strange ways to George and myself'. He is already planning a 'series of dialogues about a supposed medieval book, the *Speculum Angelorum et Hominum* by Giraldus and a sect of Arabs called the Judwalis [diagrammatists]'. It is clear that the seeds of his mystical system are already sprouting: the dialogue poems, notably *The Phases of the Moon*, which end his next volume of poetry; and his exquisite essay 'Per Amica Silentia Lunae' – the bottle from which, in Northrop Frye's phrase, the smoky genie of *A Vision* eventually issued.

But the tragic death of the poet Robert Gregory exerted an even more powerful and immediate pressure on his mind. For Gregory had embodied those manifold virtues of Renaissance man which Yeats could find so seldom in modern civilisation. Writing to Quinn he declared Gregory 'the most

accomplished man I have ever known; I mean that he could do
more things well than any other' and goes on to refer to Lady
Gregory's 'grief-stricken but courageous letters'.

Therefore when Yeats took his bride on her Irish honeymoon two months later his mind was still full of the tragedy. While staying with George at the Royal Hotel, Glendalough — he showed her Dublin and its hinterland before going west — he completed his elegy on the dead airman, 'Shepherd and Goatherd', enforcing his sense of Gregory's aristocratic excellence by writing it 'in manner like the one that Spenser wrote for Sir Philip Sidney'. Before the summer was out he had written the far greater poem 'In Memory of Major Robert Gregory'.

> We dreamed that a great painter had been born
> To cold Clare rock and Galway rock and thorn,
> To that stern colour and that delicate line
> That are our secret discipline
> Wherein the gazing heart doubles her might.
> Soldier, scholar, horseman, he,
> And yet he had the intensity
> To have published all to be a world's delight.

The visit to Coole was poignant, prolonged and triumphant. Lady Gregory and George took to each other immediately. The beauty of the landscape inspired Yeats not only to elegy but to that intense contemplation that we find in 'The Wild Swans at Coole' which gives its name to his next great volume of poems. Lady Gregory lent the couple Ballinamantane House from which George carried out her vigorous designs on the ancient tower with the steady help of Raftery and the sporadic exertion of the architect 'that drunken man of genius, Scott'. In a mood of wry complacency he wrote the lines which he then intended for its walls:

> I, the poet, William Yeats,
> With common sedge and broken slates
> And smithy work from the Gort Forge,

Restored this tower for my wife George;
And on my heirs I lay a curse [67]
If they should alter for the worse,
From fashion or an empty mind,
What Raftery built and Scott designed.

The symbolic resonance of the tower is already audible: its dynastic significance for his 'bodily heirs' and its place in the historic landscape. To Quinn he writes of it as 'a setting for my old age, a place to influence lawless youth, with its severity and antiquity'. He goes on to note that in *The Little Review* another Irishman of genius has made a tower the setting of a great novel: 'It is an entirely new thing — neither what the eye sees nor the ear hears, but what the rambling mind thinks and imagines from moment to moment.' In time he will pass on from Joyce's to Shelley's and Milton's towers as he infuses his new home with cumulative meaning:

I declare this tower is my symbol; I declare
This winding, gyring, spiring treadmill of a stair is
    my ancestral stair;
That Goldsmith and the Dean, Berkeley and Burke have
    travelled there.

Though the long summer seems to have been not only idyllic but productive it was not without its ominous side. Yeats, planning a series of Abbey lectures, wrote to Clement Shorter for permission to quote from his wife's poems in his own lecture on war poetry. In a subsequent letter (17 May) he cancelled the lecture because of the mood of the people — 'the times are too dangerous for me to encourage men to take risks I am not prepared to share or approve.' When the Yeatses went back to Dublin in October they stayed at 73 Stephen's Green which Maud Gonne had lent them. The city was turbulent with the prospect of conscription and with the general election looming at the end of the year in which the revolutionary Sinn Fein was to win hands down. Maud managed to break out of her British jail and return to Dublin.

When she appeared at the door of her house she was refused
entry by her sitting tenant and former lover on the grounds
that his wife was pregnant and suffering from influenza. A raid
by the police might upset her. George, all unknowing, proceeded with her recovery while Maud strode off angrily into the
curfew.

The row was soon settled and the Yeatses moved further
along the Green to number 96 where they were living when
Anne was born on 24 February 1919. When summer came
round the family returned to Ballylee and moved into the
Tower which was becoming increasingly habitable. It was
there, against a background of mounting violence, that he
wrote 'A Prayer for my Daughter'. The fierce sense of protect-
iveness and dread that informs the two opening stanzas as he
contemplates the child under its 'cradle-hood and coverlid'
is occasioned by the storm outside which in turn symbolises
the violent winds of change sweeping eastern Europe and the
more intimate horrors of guerilla warfare in the Gort countryside.

> I have walked and prayed for this young child an hour
> And heard the sea-wind scream upon the tower,
> And under the arches of the bridge, and scream
> In the elms above the flooded stream;
> Imagining in excited reverie
> That the future years had come,
> Dancing to a frenzied drum,
> Out of the murderous innocence of the sea.

The figure of Maud which had permeated the love poems in
The Wild Swans — 'Her Praise', 'The People', 'His Phoenix',
'Broken Dreams' — is dramatically overborne in the stanzas
that follow by the gentler quality of his wife. For Anne he
desires undemonstrative beauty, 'natural kindness', 'courtesy',
the 'radical innocence' that comes from settled, ceremonious
living.

> May she become a flourishing hidden tree

That all her thoughts may like the linnet be,
And have no business but dispensing round
Their magnanimities of sound,
Nor but in merriment begin a chase,
Nor but in merriment a quarrel.
O may she live like some green laurel
Rooted in one dear perpetual place.

This fervent aspiration may well arise from his memory of his mother's unhappy itinerant life. More immediately it must refer to his recent images of Maud moving distractedly between France, England and Ireland, railing at customs officials, harried by police, ranting from platforms, standing a fugitive at her own doorway.

An intellectual hatred is the worst,
So let her think opinions are accursed.
Have I not seen the loveliest woman born
Out of the mouth of Plenty's horn,
Barter that horn and every good
By quiet natures understood
For an old bellows full of angry wind?

There is a hint of exorcism in this vehement dismissal of Maud's restless commitment to her many causes. But the positive side of the poem's theme is to loom larger as Yeats moved towards his next and greatest volume *The Tower*: this is his sense of great houses, artifacts, values under threat from hostile historical process, 'ingenious, lovely things', the work of centuries falling before a new levelling barbarism and his fears for the generation, his 'bodily heirs' among them, who must live on amid their vacancy or ruin.

George Yeats's first visit to Ireland had lasted all of eighteen months and the evidence shows that she enjoyed it. Her husband was not only happy during this period but intensely busy both with his writing and his theatre business. It is perhaps a measure of his new tranquility that he can now advise Lady Gregory to let the younger people at the Abbey take over more of the responsibility: 'the sooner some young man, who feels that his own future is bound up with the Abbey, is put in charge the better'. Having turned to the more esoteric Noh play himself he no longer qualified on either count. In October 1919 he moved for the winter to 4 Broad Street, Oxford with his wife and daughter.

As soon as the family had settled into their Oxford home Yeats embarked on a lecture tour of the US 'to earn a roof for Thoor Ballylee'. George travelled with him, leaving Anne in the care of his sisters. The tour was successful and extensive, lasting to the middle of May. In New York he spent some time with his father – their last meeting before the old man's death – and found him as vigorous and optimistic as ever, toiling on at the self-portrait which Quinn had commissioned years before and never getting it finished. By this time Yeats was making enough money on sales and lectures to take over complete responsibility for his father's support.

On their return to Oxford the Yeatses became the centre of a cheerful literary circle. Their Monday evenings at Broad Street were frequented by dons, writers and such brilliant undergraduates as L. A. G. Strong and Maurice Bowra who was later to devote a seminal essay on Yeats in his book on poetic symbolism. Yeats delighted in the Bodleian Library, its great resources and the friendliness of its atmosphere. His old friends Robert Bridges and Sturge Moore lived within walking distance. At weekends he was invited to Lady Ottoline Morrell's great house at Garsington which is undoubtedly evoked with its terraces and peacocks in the opening of 'Meditations in Time and of Civil War'. In February 1921 Yeats was asked to speak at the Oxford Union to the motion: 'That this House would welcome self-government for Ireland and condemns reprisals'. The poet had been to Ireland the previous year for a tonsilectomy – his instructors had counselled him against London – and was vividly briefed on the atrocities of the Black and Tans. His speech at the Union denounced Britain for loosing this drunken, hysterical soldiery on Ireland, praised Sinn Féin and called for Irish self-government. His oratorical style, striking gestures and vehement utterance seem to have earned him tumultuous applause. The motion was carried by a large majority.

Oxford proved conducive to Yeats's researches in Egyptian and Indian spiritualism necessary for the building of his 'system' round the revelations of his wife's Instructors. The figures of Robartes and Ahern, long laid to rest in his early fictions, began to revive as mediums for his speculations on the phases of the moon. Indeed Robartes's prototype was resurrected — much to the dismay of his widow — in the autobiographical narrative *The Trembling of the Veil* (1922). His ghost was summoned in 'All Souls' Night', Yeats's Oxford poem *par excellence*, together with the shades of Horton and Florence Emery (Farr) who ended her days in a Buddhist seminary in Ceylon.

> And I call up MacGregor from the grave,
> For in my first hard springtime we were friends,
> Although of late estranged.
> I thought him half a lunatic, half knave,
> And told him so, but friendship never ends;

Their second child Michael was born at Cuttlebrook House, Thame, in August 1921. His parents had been getting frequent psychic vibrations from the various houses they occupied that summer and were especially gratified that there was a fragrance of roses in the room when their son was born, even though roses were then out of season.

Though Yeats was happy at Oxford he remained obsessed with Ireland, with thoughts on its current miseries and on its future possibilities. This concern united him again with Russell, from whom he had been somewhat estranged, as they planned a tract on the subject of unity of culture for the Cuala Press. He wanted to live in Ireland, yet was afraid that it would be all 'blood and misery'. If the children were brought up there they would inherit bitterness; if they remained in England it would produce an 'unnatural condition of mind' and make them like 'so many Irishmen who live

here ... sour and argumentive'.[38] George, whose desire to
live in Ireland was even greater, carried the day, having
'finally revolted against the dons' wives, their hats being the
principal offence'. While she was in Dublin searching for a
house the poet's father died in New York on 3 February
1922. George returned victorious to Oxford having secured
a large house, 82 Merrion Square with 'great eighteenth
century Dublin rooms'. She brought with her Lily Yeats
who was ill and distressed over her father's death. When
the Yeatses moved into Merrion Square in September 1922
the Irish Civil War was at its fiercest. The following month
he wrote to Olivia Shakespear of the sense of uncertainty
created by the warfare, the incendiary activities of the
Republican side, the 'drift towards Conservatism, perhaps
towards Autocracy'.

> We are entering on the final and most dreadful stage.
> Perhaps there is nothing so dangerous to a modern state,
> when politics take the place of theology, as a bunch of
> martyrs. A bunch of martyrs (1916) were the bomb and we
> are living in the explosion.

The fact that he had done much to canonize the patriots of
the Easter Rising gives urgency to his great *Tower* poem of
the period 'Meditations in Time of Civil War' written during
that summer while he lived with his wife and children at
Thoor Ballylee. His remarkable letters to Olivia — who now
carried the various honours of being the poet's ex-mistress and
friend, aunt to his wife and godmother to his son Michael —
reveal a proud and affectionate husband and father, lyrically
happy with his house and work, alive to every nuance of
rumour and action in the troubled countryside, nervous and
fascinated with the reality of war in 'this stormbeaten place'
and wondering 'will literature be much changed by that most
momentous of events, the return of evil'.

The poem's movement, at once massive and agile, turns
upon these themes with the question of evil at its centre. In
probing its subject it dwells with minute particularity upon the

daily circumstance of the poet's life: the reality and symbol of tower, house, stream, bridge, thorn, rose, bridge, starling, [73] soldier. Its stately opening movement 'Ancestral Houses' celebrates the 'inherited glory of the rich', the manor house which is the emblem of civilised living, but which was first raised by 'violent and bitter men'. But when the violence and bitterness recede with generations of peace does the greatness depart also? The question is a universal one but for Yeats, holding out in his isolated tower among deserted manor houses of the Anglo-Irish, it has a sharp immediacy. The six lyric movements that follow are the poet's response to this enigma: 'My House', 'My Table', 'My Descendants', 'The Road to my Door' and the culminating movement where the return of evil is dramatised in terrible omens of apocalypse.

The spare images that delineate his 'house' make it clear that his life and his poetry are one, a deliberate challenge to the times.

> An ancient bridge, and a more ancient tower,
> A farmhouse that is sheltered by its wall,
> An acre of stony ground
> Where the symbolic rose can break in flower.

The 'winding stair' leads to such a chamber as *'Il Penseroso's* Platonist' occupied. The bare facts of the Tower's history for Yeats and his family yield 'Befitting emblems of adversity'.

On the table lies Sato's sword, a complex symbol of art, war and aristocratic tradition; at the poem's end it has become a 'glittering sword out of the east', a portent of apocalypse. In 'My Descendants' the poet voices an anxiety which is to re-echo through his poems, plays and prefaces, but most overtly in his famous Senate speech on divorce: the survival of the Anglo-Irish, 'one of the great stocks of Europe', here epitomised by the poet and his family: 'I must nourish dreams / And leave a woman and a man behind / As vigorous of mind.' But in a sweep of bitter rhetoric he faces the possibility that history may cancel it all.

And what if my descendants lose the flower
Through natural declension of the soul,
Through too much business with the passing hour,
Through too much play, or marriage with a fool?
May this laborious stair and this stark tower
Become a roofless ruin that the owl
May build in the cracked masonry and cry
Her desolation to the desolate sky.

It is only in the fifth movement that the Civil War breaks in
with visitors from both factions: an 'affable Irregular' from the
Republican side and 'a brown Lieutenant' from the Free State
army. As the poet turns towards his chamber he feels the
ancient Johnsonian 'envy' of the man who has never been a
soldier, a thought that recurs more feverishly in the last movement when with 'wits astray' he almost joins the cry for
vengeance on Jacques Molay's[39] legendary murderers. But the
poem's crisis is in its sixth lyric where he prays that the honey-
bees — emblematic of love and peace — will come to inhabit
the deserted nest of the stare. It is a most poignant moment of
autobiography for the man who had seen war as terrible beauty
five years before.

We are closed in, and the key is turned
On our uncertainty; somewhere
A man is killed, or a house burned,
Yet no clear fact to be discerned:
Come build in the empty house of the stare.

A barricade of stone or of wood;
Some fourteen days of civil war;
Last night they trundled down the road
That dead young soldier in his blood:
Come build in the empty house of the stare.

We had fed the heart on fantasies,
The heart's grown brutal from the fare;
More substance in our enmities
Than in our love; O honey-bees,
Come build in the empty house of the stare.

For the rest of his life Yeats struggled with these great themes of violence and civilisation, heroism and brutality and with [75] his own role as a man of words, at turns exultant and guilt-ridden, in a drama that has been taken over by men of action.

Yeats would therefore have heard with mixed feelings the exchange between an unnamed politician and Oliver Gogarty when he was nominated to the Senate of the Free State Parliament. The politician questioned the right of a mere poet to legislate for the Irish Free State to which Gogarty replied: 'If it were not for the poet Yeats, there would be no Irish Free State.' Yeats accepted the honour and for the next six years vigorously discharged its attendant responsibilities. He was well aware of the risks involved.

The Senate first sat on 11 December 1922. On 30 November the Republicans had announced a policy of assassinating Senators and Deputies of the new parliament — along with twelve other hostile 'categories' — and had carried out their threats by killing Deputy Seán Hales in a Dublin street. Cosgrave's cabinet struck back by executing four prominent Republican prisoners, one from each province, which halted the assassinations but gave rise to attacks on property, especially the property of those Senators who represented the more affluent among the Anglo-Irish population. Sir Horace Plunkett, the Earl of Mayo, the Earl of Granard, Maurice Moore — brother of George Moore — the Persses of Roxborough, Lady Gregory's family, even Gogarty himself, all had houses burned down. Elected representatives had an armed body-guard.

6
'No Petty People'

Yeats gave his first Senate speech on 12 December 1922 in support of the proposal of Lord Glenavy as Cathaoirleach (Chairman) of the House. Glenavy, an outstanding lawyer, was a Unionist, had been an opponent of Home Rule and was thought by some an unhappy choice in view of his dissent from nationalist sentiment through the country. Yeats brushed aside the question of 'popularity' in favour of legal and political ability: 'What enemy of ours will lay down his gun because of any man we appoint here? I suggest we are assembled here no longer in a Nationalist or Unionist sense but merely as members of the Seanad.'[40] His old shrewdness advised him to make the Gaelic title of the House his final word.

The turbulent politics of the new state absorbed much of his energies and his Senate speeches range over a large area of concern. In 1923 he spoke nineteen times, most notably on law enforcement, Irish manuscripts, the Lane pictures, film censorship and the Irish language. His stance was mostly practical, what might be called liberal-conservative in orientation. His allies were a group of Protestant unionists – whom he may have wanted to influence in a national direction – led by his father's friend, Andrew Jameson.

In his speech on law enforcement on 8 February 1923 Yeats warns against the extension of the right of officers to enter private houses and adds a revealing anecdote about an official who had called to serve a summons on him in Co. Galway.

He had with him seven Free State soldiers to protect him. I invited him to tea, and he and the Free State soldiers had tea with me, and my wife took their photographs. Shortly afterwards, however, he found himself amongst debtors who were less hospitable, for instead of giving him tea and cake and taking his photograph, they compelled him to eat all his own summonses. There was a large quantity of paper, and paper, I believe, is extremely indigestible.

When on 14 March 1923 a bill came before the House to make provision for the family of Arthur Griffith, Yeats's old antagonist of the *Playboy* controversy, the poet paid the dead statesman an eloquent tribute: 'He gave his faith, not to an abstract theory, but to the conception of this historical nation — we are all theory mad.'

Yeats regarded his first year in the Senate as one of the most rewarding of his life. Within a week of his appointment, in December 1922, he had been given an honorary D. Litt. by Dublin University. His house at Merrion Square was the resort of politicians as well as writers: 'Here one works at the slow exciting work of creating the institutions of a new nation. . . . Meanwhile the country is full of arms and explosives ready for any violent hand to use.' The bridge at Thoor Ballylee had been blown up, filling the ground floor of the tower with water and there were already two bullet holes in the window of 82 Merrion Square.

My armed guard very much on the alert just now, (many republicans are I think in town for a conference) and I was challenged last night on the stairs. I was in my stocking feet so as not to wake the children. I give my guard detective stories to train him in the highest traditions of their profession.[41]

When he got news of the Nobel Prize award in November he was pleased because of the 'honour', the 'money' — he would now be a 'tower of strength to his ailing sister' — and because he had a 'better chance of being listened to here in Dublin than ever before'.

In December he travelled to Sweden to receive the prize
[78] making a fine impression for the grace and ceremony with
which he accepted it from the hands of the monarch. The
lessons of Castiglione had been well learned and he was
gratified to hear later that the royal family had liked him
better than any previous Nobel Prize winner because he had
'the manners of a courtier'. He chose as his theme in replying
to the honour the Irish theatre and typically insisted on
paying tribute to his collaborators.

> When your King gave me medal and diploma, two forms
> should have stood, one on either side of me, an old woman
> sinking into infirmity of age and a young man's ghost. I
> think when Lady Gregory and John Synge's names are
> spoken by future generations, my name, if remembered
> will come up in the talk, and if my name is spoken first
> their names will come in their turn because of the years
> we worked together.[42]

He went on to speak of the Abbey and its current plight
after the adverse effects of war and political unrest: 'It is too
soon yet to say what will come to us from the melodrama and
tragedy of the last four years, but if we can pay our players
and keep our theatre open something will come.' While he
dropped his solemn hint — he was always a fisher of funds —
he cannot have been indifferent to that tragic melodramatist,
Seán O'Casey, whose *Shadow of a Gunman* had played to
packed houses the previous April. And when Yeats went on
to suggest that his lecture 'ends in the middle or even, perhaps
at the beginning of the story' he is mixing a little history with
hope and prophesy. The 'House Full' notice had been hung
out on the last night of O'Casey's play and when in the following year *Juno and the Paycock* was extended for an
unprecedented second week it was clear that the miracle for
which the theatre had waited had arrived.

Back in Dublin Yeats divided his time between politics,
literature, theatre management and his wife's automatic
writing. As the first version of his 'system', later to be

formalised in *A Vision*, took shape he spent his days 'codifying fragments of philosophy' — arcane philosophy of the occult and mystical, not the modern political philosophy which was to re-shape the system after its first appearance in 1925.

On the legislative side one of his most striking speeches was on the subject of Northern Ireland and its partition from the Free State. He urged the State to woo the northern counties, suggesting that President Cosgrave 'should make another appeal to the North to meet him in counsel'. He went on

> I have no hope of seeing Ireland united in my time, or of seeing Ulster won in my time; but I believe it will be won in the end, and not because we fight it, but because we govern this country well. We can do that, if I may be permitted as a writer and an artist to say so, by creating a system of culture which will represent the whole of this country and which will draw the imagination of the young towards it.

The money from the Nobel Prize enabled the Yeatses to embark on the most extended holiday of their lives in November 1924. They travelled first to Sicily and then spent two months in the company of Ezra and Dorothy Pound who were living at Rapallo. Yeats delighted in the sunlight, in the historic architecture and the Byzantine mosaics of Palermo and Monreale. Pound's conversation was as radical as ever on art and aesthetics, more rigidly authoritarian on history and politics. The only friction was between their temperaments where Pound was beginning to evince that eccentricity which was to be his ruin in late middle age. Coming home Yeats visited Capri where he seems to have completed work on *A Vision*. The dedication of the book, Capri, February 1925, is to Mathers's widow, Vestigia: 'your beauty and your learning and your mysterious gifts were held by all in affection.' Recalling the Golden Dawn he suggested that some 'were looking for spiritual happiness or for some form of unknown power' but that he himself had a more practical object: 'I

wished for a system of thought that would leave my
[80] imagination free to create as it chose and yet make all that it
created, or could create, part of one history, that of the soul's.'

The same historical imagination fed avidly on every 'monument of unageing intellect' that he encountered as he proceeded to Rome on a tour vividly similar to his Italian visit with
the Gregories in 1907. In Rome, Michael Angelo's 'Sistine roof'
yielded him an emblem of human magnificence that was to
enliven his poetic imagination through his final years. He was
further impressed with Mussolini's new state, with the theories
of his education minister, Gentile, which he later advocated in
the Irish Senate and with the doctrines of Croce whose ideas
were absorbed into the second version of *A Vision* in 1937.

By May 1925 Yeats was back at Ballylee preparing his
celebrated speech on divorce which he delivered to a puzzled
Senate on 11 June. This oration was so counterproductive in
practical terms, and so exquisitely embarrassing to his Protestant and largely conservative colleagues, that a covert sense
of mischief on the poet's part cannot be ruled out. He could
hardly have expected his Catholic listeners to be softened by
a preamble pointing out that the statues of Parnell and Nelson
in O'Connell Street commemorated adulterers and even less by
the suggestion that O'Connell himself had been so promiscuous
that 'you could not throw a stick over a work-house wall
without hitting one of his children.' One can imagine Jameson
and Glenavy squirming in their seats as they heard themselves
eulogised in these resounding – and all too earnest – terms:

> We against whom you have done this thing are no petty
> people. We are one of the great stocks of Europe. We are
> the people of Burke; we are the people of Grattan; we are
> the people of Swift, the people of Emmet and the people
> of Parnell. We have created most of the modern literature
> of this country. We have created the best of its political
> intelligence.... If we have not lost our stamina then your
> victory will be brief, and your defeat final, and when it
> comes this country will be transformed.

The speech, curiously reminiscent (especially in its peroration) of Pearse's over the grave of Rossa, is arrogantly divisive and the Utopia it looks to could hardly have commended itself to a nation of tenant farmers whose forbears had been struggling for more than a century against the oppression of Ascendency landlordism.

Though the speech was unpopular with almost everyone and the cause lost, it can be seen in hindsight as a necessary and definitive utterance on Yeats's part at this time of his creative life. He saw on every side an erosion of the vision that had brought about the Irish cultural revival and of the generosity that had supplied the beauty to the terror of 1916. On every side he saw the rise of a narrow, philistine nationalism, a cautious subservience to an increasingly influential clericalism, a world where the Paudeens and the Biddies were making hay in the Sinn Féin sunburst. Not being primarily a statesman he probably opted for the prophetic rather than the political stance and statement. And part of the prophetic was the question, both local and global, of 'rule by the few or the many'. This debate is advanced in the poems that are to make up *The Tower* (1928), in *A Vision* published in the same year as the Senate speech and most explicitly in the preface to his play *The Words upon the Window-Pane* in which the spirit of Swift, champion of rule by the 'few', is poignantly evoked.

Yeats's collected Senate speeches reveal a man who went boldly and shrewdly through what he called 'these intricate' and 'thorny political questions', convinced of the importance of the work he had been appointed to do. He spoke with eloquence and common sense on education, prisons, the judiciary and especially on the coinage where he chaired the committee that gave the new state the most distinguished set of coins in Europe. By and large he encouraged what he tended to call 'authoritative government', feeling that only strong policies would bring peace and order to the fledgling state. He admired Kevin O'Higgins – 'A great man in his pride / Confronting murderous men' – who as Minister for

Justice had signed the execution orders of 1922 and who was to suffer assassination in July 1927. His brother, Jack B. Yeats, favoured the other side, admiring de Valera whom the poet disliked at first and later came to admire.

In February 1926 the Dublin career of Seán O'Casey reached its climax with the presentation of his greatest play, *The Plough and the Stars*. His depiction of Irish reality under political and social change had made him a fascination and a challenge to the sensibility of Dublin theatre goers. With the *Plough* the tension broke. National sentiment erupted in a manner weirdly reminiscent of the *Playboy* riots twenty years before. This time Yeats made it a point to be there. One can sense his satisfaction when he says to Gabriel Fallon: 'I'm sending for the police; and *this time* it'll be their own police.' As the rioters were being brought under control he strode onto the stage for a last great performance.

> You have disgraced yourselves again. Is this to be an ever-recurring celebration of the arrival of Irish genius? Synge first and then O'Casey. The news of the happenings of the past few minutes will go from country to country. Dublin has once more rocked the cradle of genius. From such a scene in this theatre went forth the fame of Synge. Equally the fame of O'Casey is born here tonight. This is his apotheosis.[43]

The occasion of the disturbance was a scene at the end of Act II where three revolutionary soldiers carry the tricolour into a public house and drink a tense toast to Ireland. The opposition to the play was led by Maud Gonne and the widow of Francis Sheehy-Skeffington who had been murdered by a British officer as a result of his attempts to stop the looting in Easter Week.

In the subsequent newspaper controversy Mrs Skeffington expressed her indignation 'against the outrage of a drama staged in a supposedly national theatre, which held up to derision and obloquy the men and women of Easter Week'. O'Casey defended himself ably in the pages of the *Irish*

Independent but made the mistake of accepting her challenge to a debate which took place on 1 March at Mills Hall. O'Casey, due to nerves and illness, gave a poor account of himself but Yeats — now not only the author of *Cathleen ni Houlihan* but of 'Easter 1916' was at his pugnacious best: 'At no time, neither in the beginning nor its final maturity, does an intellectual movement express a whole people, or anybody but those who are built into it, as a victim long ago was built into the foundations of a bridge.'[44] Privately Yeats was exhilarated. Writing to Olivia Shakespear he is convinced that the 'theatre has now a great following', that 'minds have been suddenly liberated from hereditary political passions. . . . I feel constantly if I were but twenty years old and not over sixty all I ever wanted to do could be done easily. One never tires of life and at the last must die of thirst with the cup at one's lip.'

One of his own most successful dramatic enterprises took place in the same year: his version of *King Oedipus* based on a variety of translations including that of his old friend, Sir Gilbert Murray. Its cathartic effect on a poet so obsessed by Greece, myth and tragedy is readily understood. Added tension is provided by the fact that the play was banned in England because of its theme of incest, but permissible in Dublin to which the Lord Chamberlain's Act did not extend. To Olivia Shakespear Yeats wonders 'how will the Catholics take it?' Watching it in final rehearsal he feels nothing 'but one overwhelming emotion, a sense of the actual presence in a terrible sacrament of the god'. So well did the play succeed that by the end of the year Yeats was at work on its sequel, *Oedipus at Colonus* which was performed at the Abbey in September of the following year 1927. During its performance Yeats and George were infuriated by the barking of a dog which seemed to come from the gallery. No dog could be discovered. The poet recalled with resignation that one of the play's choruses 'appeals to Cerberus not to disturb Oedipus with its barking'.[45] The actors however were convinced that it was the bark of a dog which had been accidentally locked in and died during the closed season. Yeats, scholar of the ghostly Noh, was equally satisfied with that.

At the end of 1927 Yeats went with George on an extended tour of Spain, France and Italy. At Seville the poet suffered an attack of bleeding of the lungs. His wife hurried him to the south of France where the doctors at Cannes brought the condition under control. During his recovery in February 1928 *The Tower* was published to universal critical acclaim. Apart from 'Meditations in Time of Civil War' which has already been considered at length, the book contained some of his most searching and powerful explorations of contemporary history. 'Nineteen Hundred and Nineteen' – whose title suggests continuity with 'September 1913' and 'Easter 1916' – displays, together with the great title poem, Yeats's mastery of the varied lyric sequence, his unique vehicle for the expression of complex personal and political thought. 'Leda and the Swan' and 'Two Songs from a Play' dramatise with staggering force separate apocalyptic moments in western history when civilisation was reversed by the incarnational force of the godhead. With the rape of Leda by Zeus, Helen and Claetemestra are begotten and a whole dynastic world comes to grief in the rhetoric of two and a half tremendous lines.

> A shudder in the loins engenders there
> The broken wall, the burning roof and tower
> And Agamemnon dead.

In 'Two Songs', with almost equal concentration of word and image, Christ, – born of the mild virgin – dies while Pallas Athene holds on her hand the heart of Dionysus as a proleptic image of a new era brutally conceived:

> The Roman Empire stood appalled:
> It dropped the reins of peace and war
> When that fierce virgin and her Star
> Out of the fabulous darkness called.

The volume shudders with apocalyptic force as epoch calls to epoch and the poet seeks to embody that sense of 'the soul's history' which he had tried to frame in *A Vision*. Thus in 'Nineteen Hundred and Nineteen' Loie Fuller's Chinese dancers at the Follies Bergeres produce the illusion of a dragon when they unwind their 'shining ribbon of cloth' and present the poet with yet another protean image of human destiny.

> It seemed that a dragon of air
> Had fallen among dancers, had whirled them round
> Or hurried them off on its own furious path;
> So the Platonic Year
> Whirls out new right and wrong,
> Whirls in the old instead
> All men are dancers and their tread
> Goes to the barbarous clangour of a gong.

The orchestration of his large public themes are deftly offset within the volume by a number of exquisite personal poems on love, art and mutability — 'Sailing to Byzantium', 'The New Faces', 'Among School Children' and the lyric sequence, 'A Man Young and Old'. Though he had far from recovered his strength, Yeats was nevertheless a victorious poet as he moved from Cannes to Rapallo to visit his fellow craftsman, Ezra Pound.

It was at Rapallo that the Yeatses made a number of important decisions and changes in their life pattern. George left her convalescent husband with Dorothy and Ezra Pound and took the two children to a Swiss boarding school. On her return she secured a flat on the Via Americhe for their future winter residence at Rapallo. They determined to put their Dublin house on the market and look for a more modest home in the city. Yeats decided to give up the Senate the better to devote his diminished energies to writing.

On their way home they called on Michael at Villars-sur-Box and found him 'more vigorous and self-reliant'. When they asked him to lunch with them on Easter Sunday 'he said he was not sure as he did not yet know what the school would have for lunch but would find out.' By mid-April Yeats and George were back in Merrion Square. Within a week

Yeats had dispatched that disastrous letter of rejection to
Seán O'Casey having read the script of *The Silver Tassie*. The
opening words 'Dear Casey' and the rather lofty, travelled
tone of an otherwise conscientious analysis so annoyed the
sensitive, younger man that he severed his connection with
the Abbey and was not reconciled with the poet for seven
years. Part of Yeats's failure in tact may have been his
impatience with O'Casey's pacifist socialist ideology and his
pretension to deal with large contemporary movements. 'But
you are not interested in the great war', Yeats assures him.
Such momentous affairs are, implicitly, best left to his betters.
Yeats, after all, has the historic perspective in hand as he
shapes the final version of *A Vision*.

That summer of 1928 was a restless time for the poet.
Having sold 82 Merrion Square he moved in July to a rented
house at Howth, scene of many happy childhood memories.
From there he wrote to Lady Gregory that he had made his
last appearance in the Senate: 'A little speech, three sentences,
was followed by a minute of great pain.' He regretted the loss
to his family of the salary, £360 a year and regretted even
more his inability now to oppose the new Censorship of
Publications Act on the floor of the House. But he determined
to 'fight the censorship' in two newspaper interviews before
his winter departure to Rapallo. By August the family had
moved into their new, comfortable flat at 42 Fitzwilliam
Square. Yeats had almost completed *A Packet for Ezra Pound*
– later to be incorporated in *A Vision* – which fittingly
received its final shape in his friend's presence at Rapallo. It
was published the following year by his sister's Cuala Press.

After an easy winter in the sun Yeats returned to Fitzwilliam
Square via London where he renewed his friendship with
Olivia Shakespear and Charles Ricketts. He had tea with
Wyndham Lewis whose *Time and Western Man* had been his
absorbing interest for at least two years. But this meeting
of right-wing prophets yielded little to either: 'Both too
cautious, with too much sympathy for one another not to
fear we might discover some fundamental difference. We

played with all topics and said as little as possible.'[46]

Back in Ireland he divided his time between Coole, Dublin and Ballylee which he occupied for the last time as its dampness and isolation no longer suited his failing health. The climax of his summer was the Abbey production of his dance play, *Fighting the Waves*, with Ninette de Valois playing Fand, the Woman of the Shee. He regarded it as his 'greatest success since Kathleen-ni-Houlihan' and believed that he had discovered 'a new form by this dance, speech and music'. It has taken forty years or more of theatrical experiment to prove him right.

When he returned in the winter to Rapallo he suffered a severe attack of Maltese fever which brought about total collapse. During his slow convalescence, having exhausted his store of detective novels, he conceived a passion for stories of the Wild West. It is reported that in the midst of a fever he woke up shouting, 'Send for the Sheriff!' When he was strong enough George took him to a hotel among the mountains of Portofino Vetto where the air and the scenery revived his health and his old passion for work. With summer the children came to Rapallo and the family was together in what seems to have been blissful domesticity. In a letter to Olivia the poet chuckles at the children's squabbles over chess and pities the Pounds for being separated from their son: 'Michael had his two hands in Anne's hair, and Anne was pounding Michael. The point was – had Michael checkmated Anne. What a lot Dorothy is missing by leaving Omar in London!'

On his return to Ireland in the late summer of 1930 he stayed for some time with Lady Gregory at Coole where he prepared *The Words Upon the Window Pane* for its successful autumn production at the Abbey. He felt strong enough to spend the winter in Ireland where he began work again on a project which had obsessed him on and off since his return from Sweden, the founding of an Irish Academy of Letters. The passing of the Censorship Act had convinced him that writers needed a forum, 'an organ through which we can address the public, or appeal collectively and unanimously to the Government'.[47]

While the academy project was germinating in his mind Yeats was offered an honorary doctorate by Oxford University which he travelled to receive in May 1931; Cambridge followed suit in 1933. By the end of 1931, following long discussions at Coole with Lady Gregory – now in her last year of life – he had put together his scheme for the Academy. Together with Shaw who primed the pump with a donation of £50, he set about drawing up a list of prospective members with a circular letter of invitation outlining the scope and role of the proposed body. By April 1932 the joint Shaw-Yeats letter was ready for the post and Yeats was preparing for a fund-raising tour of America to promote the aims of the Academy. On 22 May Lady Gregory died. Hearing that she was near death Yeats took the first train to Galway and arrived to find that she had died in the night, 'her indomitable self to the last but of that I will not write, or not now'.[48] His tears were not yet brewed but would soon issue in the noble Coole Park elegies of *The Winding Stair*. It was a time for elegy: O'Higgins had been murdered, and the friends of his youth the Gore-Booth sisters had died, Eva in 1926, Constance Markievicz in the year following. In July of 1932 Yeats stayed at the Royal Hotel, Glendalough amid memories of his honeymoon while George with her 'fine taste' prepared for the last time a new family house, Riversdale, 'just too far from Dublin to go there without good reason and too far, I hope, for most interviewers and the less determined travelling bores'.

The first meeting of the Academy took place on 14 September 1932 with the election of Shaw as president, Yeats as vice-president and A.E. as secretary. A month later Yeats set out on his lecture tour of the US and by early January he had collected £600 for himself and an equal amount for the Academy. While Yeats lived and for some years after his death the Academy played a salient role in Irish cultural affairs, instituting three awards, the Harmsworth, the Casement and the O'Curry Awards and the Gregory Gold Medal. Much of its success was due to American friends: Judge Richard Campbell, James A. Farrell and Yeats's old friend the Fenian Dr Patrick McCartan who was guest of honour at their 1937 banquet and was presented with the prototype of the Gregory Medal. It was a distinguished body numbering Gogarty, James Stephens, Francis Stuart, Edith Somerville, Frank O'Connor, Seán O'Faolain and Liam O'Flaherty among its members and exotically Eugene O'Neill and Lawrence of Arabia among its associates. Those who refused are even more interesting – James Joyce, Seán O'Casey, George Moore, Stephen McKenna, Lord Dunsany and Daniel Corkery.

The Winding Stair (1933) is a gentler book than the *Tower* volume. It is at once elegiac and life-affirming and with the exception of the savage 'Blood and the Moon' largely free of the violent and sometimes feverish political debate that permeates his two remaining volumes. The opening poem on the Gore-Booth sisters recalls the graciousness of a previous age symbolised by the great house and 'Two girls in silk kimonos, both / Beautiful, one a gazelle'. The 'raging autumn' which has marred the dynastic promise of Lissadell is also at work in Coole where Yeats conjures the presence of 'an ancient woman and her house' in the last days when Lady Gregory was confined to two rooms.

> Sound of a stick upon the floor, a sound
> Of somebody that toils from chair to chair;
> Beloved books that famous hands have bound,
> Old marble heads, old pictures everywhere;
> Great rooms where travelled men and children found
> Content and joy; a last inheritor
> Where none has reigned that lacked a name and fame
> Or out of folly into folly came.

In her final years the state Forestry Department bought Coole Park and rented back the house to Lady Gregory, its 'last inheritor', for her lifetime. When she died it was sold to a purchaser who had it demolished in 1941. It remains a puzzle that

Yeats, who had espoused so many such causes, did not lead an
agitation to save the house he had so revered and celebrated.
Instead he contented himself with a poignant prophecy of its
dissolution in lines like these:

> Here, traveller, scholar, poet, take your stand
> When all these rooms and passages are gone,
> When nettles wave upon a shapeless mound
> And saplings root among the broken stone ...

It is frequently written of Yeats that a new erotic note sounds
in his verse after the Steinach rejuvenation operation he under-
went in 1934. This note is, however, audible in the 'Crazy
Jane' lyrics of *The Winding Stair* in which, side by side with
the stately elegies for great houses, the primitive energies and
ballad rhythms of Irish rural life again assert themselves. The
lyric sequence 'A Woman Young and Old' is a sort of antiphon
to 'A Man Young and Old' of *The Tower* where the poet had
reviewed in vivid epiphanies a lifetime of desire, frustration
and fulfilment. And in such great poems as his 'Dialogue of
Self and Soul' and 'Vacillation', poems shot through with
the philosophies he had steeped himself in since the first
version of *A Vision*, he explores and affirms the value of love
and conflict *sub specie aeternitatis*. But only in 'Blood and
the Moon' do we find a foreshadowing of the ferocity, the
'lust and rage' of his last two volumes and their passionate
concern with contemporary politics. To appreciate their
thrust and ardour it is necessary to glance briefly at *A Vision*.

The thought of apocalypse pervades Yeats's consciousness
from the days of his association with·Mathers in the 1890s.
With the rise of violence at home and abroad from 1914
onwards omen and prophecy had become fact. He had written
propagandist poems and plays and thus felt deeply implicated
in the historical process. Because he had foretold – in poems
like 'The Valley of the Black Pig' – the horror and bloodshed,
he felt the more a need to find a theory of history which
might contain and explain the present in the light of the past
and what seemed to be the future. By 1917 he had absorbed

the thought of several writers and doctrines which proposed a cyclical or apocalyptic view of history, Blake, Nietzsche, Mathers, Swedenborg and Joachim of Flora. The revelations which reached him through his wife's Instructors were not in the strict sense new: all of them could be traced to his strange voluminous reading and esoteric practices, much of which had been shared by George, herself a Rosicrucian.

The fundamental tenet of his doctrine was therefore one that he had enunciated in the stories of *The Secret Rose* and repeated in his introduction to *The Resurrection* that 'our civilisation was about to reverse itself, or some new civilisation about to be born from all that our age had rejected . . . because we had worshipped a single god it would worship many or receive from Joachim of Flora's Holy Spirit a multitudinous influx'. The signs of the consummation were everywhere but chiefly in the wars leading up to and into the 1920s and the rise of mass movements, Communism, Fascism, Nazism, on the European mainland. *A Vision* sets about reading those signs against the backdrop of history.

Through the arduous complexity of its language and symbolism the book reveals at least one simple pattern: certain periods of history seem to have been favourable for the development of human excellence and social harmony. Of these the Athens of Phidias, the Byzantine Empire and the Italian Renaissance stand out for their political culture, their cultivation of the arts and their high sense of human excellence, all of which are summarised in Yeats's term 'unity of being'. These three cultures are separated from one another by a thousand years. In Yeats's pattern, therefore, unity of being is achieved in Athens five hundred years after the fall of Troy. Having reached its peak it declines over five hundred years when it is replaced by its opposite, the Christian dispensation which replaces many gods with one and asks man for obedience to a system rather than for the exertion of his individual creativity.

The energies that make unity of being possible Yeats termed 'antithetical'; their opposite he called 'primary'. Five

hundred years after Christ the antithetical energies are again at
[92] their crest in Byzantium. As they decline the primary qualities
grow towards their zenith in the ecclesiastical discipline of
the 'didactic Middle Ages'. Five hundred years later on
'Urbino's windy hill' amid the humanism of the Renaissance
the antithetical powers create the all-round man — courtier,
scholar, horseman, poet. Four hundred years on and the
individual creative will is asked to obey the 'levelling spirit'
of twentieth century mass culture, democracy, communism,
socialism. To embody this view of history Yeats invoked the
ancient symbolism of 'gyres', or interpenetrating cones, one
primary, one antithetical, expanding and contracting as the
centuries proceed. The primary gyre in his own time is reaching its fullest extension. Soon, amid violence, it will crumble
and a new antithetical gyre begin to grow. Born into a primary
age Yeats's own antithetical personality is both active and
vigilant as the 'widening gyre' of contemporary history moves
towards millenial crisis.

Any assessment of Yeats's politics — his 'flirtation with
Fascism', his 'anti-democratic prejudices', his 'delight in
violence' and so on — is meaningless without this doctrine,
whose mere skeleton I have sketched to illuminate it. Con-
versely a great deal that seems angular or perverse in his
politics becomes intelligible if the larger picture is taken into
account.

The age was desperate, the time out of joint. Hence his
respect for the eighteenth century where unity of being manifested itself in such a statesman as Lord Treasurer Harley in
comparison with whom Swift considered himself a 'poor
scholar.' In that age — a mere hundred years on from the
English Renaissance — unity of being was still possible though
somewhat over-rationalised and abstract, 'more diagram than
body'. Now, by comparison, everything is fragmented:
'philosophers are professors, their pupils compile note-books
that they may be professors some day; politicians stick to their
last or leave it to plague us with platitudes; we poets and
artists may be called, so small our share in life "separate

spirits", words applied by the old philosophers to the dead.'[49]
When he agreed to become a senator he was pleased to be part
of a body of distinguished men who would not otherwise
have been elected. And he worked hard to equip himself as
a poet-statesman, in the line of Swift, to bring the creative
imagination to bear on the profession of politics. The new
state had given a role to the intellectual elite, in Swift's phrase
'the few' and he was pleased to serve that ideal.

While composing the first version of *A Vision* Yeats refrained
from reading philosophers so as not to endanger the purity of
his revelations and their source. After its publication in 1925
however he read voraciously especially in the area of political
and historical philosophy — Vico, Croce, Gentile, Berkeley,
Spengler, Toynbee, Wyndham Lewis. He watched the world of
politics with great vigilance searching for signs of new beginnings: 'Students of contemporary Italy, where Vico's thought
is current through its influence upon Croce and Gentile, think
it created, or in part created, the present government of one
man surrounded by just such able assistants as Vico foresaw.'[50]
Perhaps the unifying power of Mussolini's programmes in Italy
might provide some model for a similar unity in Ireland. His
'Pages from a Diary in 1930' were an extended rumination
over the means of bringing the Catholic and Protestant nations
and their component classes into cultural and political unity.

> Preserve that which is living and help the two Irelands,
> Gaelic Ireland and Anglo-Ireland, so as to unite that neither
> shall shed its pride.... Study the great problems of the
> world ... the re-birth of European spirituality in the mind
> of Berkeley, the restoration of European order in the mind
> of Burke.... Study the educational system of Italy, the
> creation of the philosopher Gentile.... [51]

All of this is to be undertaken so that Ireland will be prepared
for the moment when 'the world changes and its reflection
changes in our mirror and a hieratical society returns'.

The cardinal point about Yeats's thought and activity is
that he is consciously working in an interim. The age of the

mass movements is reaching its climax and will end with a bloody Armageddon as the primary gyre implodes. The Irish must work rapidly with whatever is to hand so as to emerge from the trauma with a large role to play on the world stage. The ideology of the 'Corporate State' was emerging as one of the possibilities. In April 1933 Yeats wrote to Olivia Shakespear that he was working with 'an ex-cabinet minister, an eminent lawyer and a philosopher' to work out a theory that might be used against Communism in Ireland – 'what looks like emerging is Fascism modified by religion'. When O'Duffy 'the Fascist organiser of the Blue shirts' visits him he is well prepared, having re-written for the seventh time the 'part of *A Vision* that deals with the future'. But O'Duffy's profile did not fit that prophetic frame: he was not 'a great man' though 'his face and mind may harden and clarify'; in O'Leary's noble head the soft, boozy countenance of O'Duffy had a hard act to follow. The tone of these letters is so shot through with humorous mischief that it is hard to know how seriously Yeats is taking it all. We can see him impressing his old lover with how close he is to the centre of the action, unlike the situation in 1916 where he had not even been 'consulted'. On 20 September he constructed for her a mad scenario projecting 'our political comedy' which in three acts delivers the entire country to O'Duffy's dictatorship with 'all the opposition united under him'. Four months later he produces a vignette, domestic and political which, even in the letters of great men would be hard to match for humour, tenderness and point.

Next door is a large farm-house in considerable grounds. People called _____ live there, 'blue shirts' of local importance and until one day two weeks ago they had many dogs. 'Blue shirts' are upholding law, incarnations of public spirit, rioters in the cause of peace, and George hates 'Blue shirts'. She was delighted when she caught their collie-dog in our hen-house and missed a white hen. 'I will write to complain. If they do nothing I will go to the police.' When

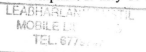

I returned in the evening she was plunged in gloom. Her letter sent by our gardener had been replied to at once in these words: 'Sorry, have done away with collie-dog' — note the Hitler touch — a little later came the gardener. In his presence, Mrs _____ had drowned four dogs. A fifth had revived, when taken out of the water, and as it was not her own dog but a stray she had hunted it down the road with a can tied to its tail. . . . I tried to console George — after all she was only responsible for the death of the collie and so on. But there was something wrong. At last it came. The white hen had returned. Was she to write and say so? I said 'No; you feel a multi-murdress and if you write, Mrs _____ will feel she is.' 'But she will see the hen.' 'Put it in the pot.' 'It is my best layer.' However I insisted and the white hen went into the pot. Yours affectionately.

7
'Horseman, pass by!'

In October 1934 Yeats was invited to take the chair at the Fourth Congress of the Alessandro Volta Foundation in Rome where again he took the opportunity of lecturing on the Irish National Theatre. His lung condition returned on his way home and he was confined to bed early in the following year. By March 1935 he was well enough to accept a commission from the Clarendon Press to edit the *Oxford Book of Modern Verse*. Amid compliments and celebrations for his seventieth birthday — 'many telegrams, and 129 signatures on vellum, and have been generally praised and petted'[52] — he worked on his controversial choices and on the proofs of *A Vision*. In the autumn he saw the dancer Margot Ruddock perform in *The Player Queen* at a festival of his plays held by Nancy Price at the People's National Theatre, London. It was at this time that Lady Ottoline Morrell introduced him to Lady Dorothy Wellesley whose poetry he was to include in the *Oxford Book*. Unlike his friendship with Margot Ruddock — which ended tragically — his association with Dorothy Wellesley, later Duchess of Wellington, was another example of those remarkable intellectual affairs with women that characterised his long career. By the end of November Yeats writes to her from Dublin:

I await Friday with longing, on that day a curtain blots out all my public life, theatre, Academy, Cuala. My work on the anthology is finished. . . . I am planning a new life, four months in every year in some distant spot and nothing to do but poetry. . . . My public life I will pare down to almost nothing. My imagination is on fire again.

He spent the winter in Majorca with the Indian monk Shri Purohit Swami whom he helped to translate the Upanishads. [97] They stayed first at the Hotel Terramar, Palma, but later moved to a villa, Casa Pastor, when the poet's health again took a bad turn. His determination to abandon politics and public life was tested by another of his intellectual women, Ethel Mannin, who tried to persuade him to recommend the German poet Ossietsky, then in a concentration camp, for the Nobel Prize. He refuses:

> Do not try to make a politician of me, even in Ireland I shall never I think be that again — as my sense of reality deepens, and I think it does with age, my horror at the cruelty of governments grows greater, and if I did what you want I would seem to hold one form of government more responsible than any other and that would betray my convictions. Communist, fascist, nationalist, clerical, anticlerical, are all responsible according to the number of their victims.

The running battle he carried on with this persistent socialist over the following years gives us a valuable insight to his current political outlook.

A more serious incursion on his privacy took the form of Margot Ruddock at his door at 6.30 a.m., 'her luggage in her hand'. She had been encouraged by Yeats's interest in her verse — some of which he had included in the *Oxford Book*— and had come from London to see if her poetry had any merit. In her crazed state of mind she went out into the pouring rain, danced on the beach, determined upon suicide so that 'her verse would live instead of her', fell through the roof of a bakery and stowed away in a ship, 'singing her own songs most of the time'.[53] Yeats and George had to travel to Barcelona and take financial responsibility for her mishaps before she was sent back to London. The incident provoked from Yeats the prosy grumble that he would not be able to afford new clothes for a year as well as two poignant lyrics, 'Sweet Dancer' and 'A Crazed Girl'.

The Yeatses were back in Riversdale by June 1936. The
poet ruefully acknowledges a new sign of old age in the fact
that Anne can now beat him at croquet, a game at which he
was exceptionally skilful. The same lawn witnessed an improb-
able rite of reconciliation in September of that year when
Yeats played croquet there with Seán O'Casey. Ever since *The
Silver Tassie* quarrel Yeats had continued to make conciliatory
overtures to the younger man. Eventually in February 1935
O'Casey wrote sympathising with the poet on his illness. In
May when Yeats visited London they dined together and the
following September, when O'Casey paid his first and last
visit to Dublin since the estrangement, he visited Riversdale
and played croquet in the afternoon. Judging from an obituary
which O'Casey wrote on the poet for a Marxist journal four
years later, Yeats must have been at his most tactful when the
conversation turned to politics, because O'Casey had found
that Yeats had become 'more human, drew nearer to the
world's needs, and as he told me himself, became intensely
interested in the new voice of the resurgent working class
speaking in its own way, and demanding the earth and the
fullness thereof. He is gone now and Ireland will miss him
sorely, for he was Ireland's greatest poet, and a great warrior
to boot.'[54]

His warrior spirit had indeed been needed when the Abbey
had belatedly put on *The Silver Tassie* a month before the
visit to Riversdale. With mixed pride and exasperation Yeats
had then written to Dorothy Wellesley of the disturbances:
'When I arrived priests, mainly country priests, were
denouncing the Abbey for blasphemy, calling on the Government to withdraw our subsidy and institute a censorship of the
stage. Our offence was producing O'Casey's *Silver Tassie*.
Meanwhile Dublin was crowding to the theatre.'

The stimulation of theatre was quickly followed by the
goad of politics. In November the Casement forgeries were
revealed, and Yeats's outrage found vent in his stark, accusing
ballad, 'Roger Casement' which he hoped would be 'sung by
Irish undergraduates at Oxford'. It was published in its

unexpurgated form in *The Irish Press* on 2 February 1937 and Mrs Yeats was first puzzled then gratified by the increased deference shown her in the Dublin shops. Once again Yeats had the nationalists on his side: *The Irish Press* in a long leader declared that his ballad would be sung 'for generations to come' and the poet was publicly thanked by de Valera's government.

After the collapse of the Blueshirt movement O'Duffy had taken the Irish brigade to fight for Franco in the Spanish Civil War. Writing to the indefatigable Ethel Mannin Yeats seems worried by the prospect of 'General O'Duffy back in Ireland with enhanced fame helping the "Catholic Front"'. On this point he need not have distressed himself. O'Duffy's brigade returned hardly having fired a shot, making history as the first expeditionary force to come home with more men than it had taken out. In 'Parnell's Funeral' Yeats mourns savagely for the kind of leadership he believed Parnell had given before being dragged down by the rabble. The current world of politics is again infected by 'the contagion of the throng'. The bloody symbolism of his malediction once more apprehended an apocalyptic sense of doom.

> The rest I pass, one sentence I unsay.
> Had de Valera eaten Parnell's heart
> No loose-lipped demagogue had won the day,
> No civil rancour torn the land apart.
>
> Had Cosgrave eaten Parnell's heart, the land's
> Imagination had been satisfied,
> Or lacking that, government in such hands,
> O'Higgins its sole statesman had not died.
>
> Had even O'Duffy — but I name no more —
> Their school a crowd, his master solitude;
> Through Jonathan Swift's dark grove he passed, and there
> Plucked bitter wisdom that enriched his blood.

He comes increasingly to the conclusion that the crust of order is cracking throughout the world, the irrational making a

bloody and triumphant return. Civilisation itself is a deception,
'is hooped together, brought / Under a rule, under a semblance
of peace / By manifold illusion'.[55] In 'The Gyres' his sense
of imminent dissolution calls up a mood of terror and fascination. Only a posture of 'tragic joy' can comfort the individual
soul as 'Irrational streams of blood' stain the earth and the
gyre sweeps outward towards its collapse:

> What matter though dumb nightmare ride on top
> And blood and mire the sensitive body stain?
> What matter? Heave no sigh, let no tear drop,
> A greater, a more gracious time has gone;
> For painted forms or boxes of make-up
> In ancient tombs I sighed, but not again;
> What matter? Out of cavern comes a voice,
> And all it knows is that one word 'Rejoice!'[56]

The cavern of history reassures the age that out of the terror
will eventually come a finer world and all things will run on
'that unfashionable gyre again'.

These powerful and sanguinary poems of the final phase —
in one he quotes with apparent relish Mitchel's prayer 'Send
war in our time, O Lord' — would be monstrous if they were
not seen against Yeats's theory of history. Fate has ordained
that he must live through one of the ugliest periods of human
process, a squalid staging-post in the movement of civilisation.
Violence is a necessary condition of change. His endorsement
of war — and it is very rare even in these last poems — is
provisional. It will hasten change and the agents of bloodshed
will be consumed in the conflict, as he asserts to Ethel Mannin:

> ...why should I trouble about communism, fascism,
> liberalism, radicalism, when all, though some bow first and
> some stern first but all at the same pace, all are going down
> stream with the artificial unity which ends every civilization?

In the meantime it is not ephemeral politics but inner vision,
wisdom drawn from poetry and tradition, that will save the
Irish soul. In 'The Statues' he attributes the victory of Salamis

to the sculptors who gave a model of heroic vision and proportion to the Greeks. Ireland, looking out upon the spawning chaos and violence of Europe, must cultivate its ancient virtues and prepare for the new age.

> When Pearse summoned Cuchulain to his side,
> What stalked through the Post Office? What intellect,
> What calculation, number, measurement, replied?
> We Irish, born into that ancient sect
> But thrown upon this filthy modern tide
> And by its formless, spawning fury wrecked,
> Climb to our proper dark that we may trace
> The lineaments of a plummet-measured face.

There is a happy symmetry in the reflection that the statue of Cuchulain he had in mind had been sculpted by his old class-mate of the Municipal School of Art, Oliver Sheppard and sited in the GPO to commemorate the Easter Rising.

Between 1937 and 1938 Yeats made a series of five successful broadcasts for the BBC. He addressed the Abbey audience for the last time in 1938 at the premiere of his play *Purgatory*. Also in 1938 he lost his great friend Olivia Shakespear. Though his health declined his creativity remained undiminished. Side by side with his global anxieties there arose in his poetry a remarkable sweetness rooted in his friendships and in the felicities of his family life:

> All his happier dreams came true —
> A small old house, wife, daughter, son,
> Grounds where plum and cabbage grew,
> Poets and Wits around him drew:

What other poet of his time could have accommodated cabbage to a Sabine idyll? The friends dropped off, one by one, among them George Russell whose remains came back from Bournemouth – in 1935 – accompanied by James Stephens and Oliver Gogarty. Yeats's refusal to give the funeral oration – 'I would have had to tell the whole truth' – has not been entirely forgiven by A.E.'s admirers.

In 1938 Yeats moved to the south of France, settling for March at the Hotel Ideal Sejour at Cap Martin. He returned to Riversdale in May where he summoned the wit and energy to write his splendid short poem 'Politics' which seems momentarily to dismiss all his fierce political apprehensions: 'But O that I were young again / And held her in my arms.'

Life at Riversdale seems to have fulfilled most of his expectations. He was not plagued by the 'travelling bores' looking for interviews, yet the 'Poets and Wits' provided his evenings with lively conversation and the right degree of homage. Captain MacManus his old Blueshirt friend called constantly: 'Shouldered his crutch and showed how fields were won' and F. R. Higgins, the bawdy extrovert poet was a constant visitor. When another friend, the austere Frank O'Connor, asked Yeats what he saw in Higgins the poet replied that at his age he needed someone to talk to him about women. Maud Gonne who had never vanished from his poems also called, her resentment of his Senate days healed if not entirely forgotten. In 1937 a group of American admirers had set up a fund to provide the poet with a modest supplement to his income for his declining years and Yeats had accepted on condition that the gift be made public. He enumerated his blessings, but without complacency:

> Everything he wrote was read,
> After certain years he won
> Sufficient money to his need,
> Friends that have been friends indeed:
> *What then? sang Plato's ghost. What then?*

Yeats had lived his life consciously between the two polarities, 'That of race and that of soul' and the two impulses were kept in tense equilibrium as he neared the end. Indeed his mood had been brilliantly foreshadowed more than thirty years before in one of the 'beggar' poems of *Responsibilities*.

> 'And there I'll grow respected at my ease
> And hear amid the garden's nightly peace,'

Beggar to beggar cried, being frenzy-struck,
'The wind-blown clamour of the barnacle geese.'

In December 1938 Yeats and George returned to the Hotel Ideal Sejour, at Cap Martin. There he worked on his last play, *The Death of Cuchulain* and his long valedictory poem, 'Under Ben Bulben'. There were several of his Irish and English friends staying in the area and his son Michael came to join them for Christmas. The poet seemed in good heath and was in excellent spirits. In a letter written on 4 January he confided to Lady Elizabeth Pelham: 'I am happy, and I think full of an energy, of an energy I had despaired of. It seems to me that I have found what I wanted. When I try to put it all into a phrase I say, "Man can embody truth but he cannot know it". I must embody it in the completion of my life.' On Thursday 26 January his health took a turn for the worse. In the evening he rallied, called George to his bedside and dictated to her some emendations to 'Under Ben Bulben'. Two days later on Saturday 28 January 1939, he died.

Political conditions in Europe prevented the return of the poet's remains to Ireland. In 1948 they were brought back to Sligo and re-interred at Drumcliff according to his wishes. The inscription on the plain limestone monument over the grave is prescribed in the poem he was composing when he died:

Under bare Ben Bulben's head
In Drumcliff churchyard Yeats is laid.
An ancestor was rector there
Long years ago, a church stands near,
By the road an ancient cross.
No marble, no conventional phrase;
On limestone quarried near the spot
By his command these words are cut:
 Cast a cold eye
 On life, on death.
 Horseman, pass by!

8

'They were my Close Companions'

In 'Among School Children' Senator W. B. Yeats stands in a
Wexford class-room, a 'sixty-year-old smiling public man',
listens to a kind old nun explain the Montessori teaching
method while his mind moves in passionate reverie over his
relationship with Maud Gonne and on the theme of mutability as experienced by nuns, mothers and three philosophers of
the soul: Plato, Aristotle and Pythagoras. It is a typically
Yeatsian moment: public occasion, private reverie, a structure
of thought conducted through a succession of *personae*,
individual and generic. In tracing the progress of Yeats's life
so far, it has been necessary to concentrate on the more overtly
public side of his career, which includes his activities among
'secret' societies. But it has not been possible to do justice
to those named relationships that so frequently enter into
the fabric of his poetry. And in few modern writers is there
such a litany of personal names.

There is first the constellation of great names out of
history from Alexander and Caesar through 'world trans-
forming Charlemagne' to Parnell and Casement. There is the
rollcall of heroic figures from mythology: Achilles, Hector,
Helen, Cuchulain, Deirdre, Diarmuid and Grania. There is
the succession of artistic exemplars from 'golden-thighed
Pythagoras' through 'gentle Phidias' Michael Angelo, Milton
and Swift to 'William Blake who beat upon the wall / Till truth
obeyed his call'. There are the philosophers and theologians
from Hermes and Plato through Joachim of Flora, Empedocles
and Swedenborg to Berkeley, Hegel, Von Hugel and 'profound
McTaggart'. Then there are the imagined personages of

literature – all 'in the Great Memory stored' – Timon and Lear, Hamlet and Cordelia, Oedipus, Don Juan and Axël, each carrying a world of significance into the poetry and each constituting a definite thematic relationship with Yeats in his role of artist.

I want to concentrate on a final set of names and relationships. These are the people he met, loved and quarrelled with and who found their way into the text of his poetry as recognisable personalities. It is important that a writer's biography should at least ask why certain of his family, friends, lovers and enemies were chosen to be named and included in his poetry, the most concentrated expression of his imaginative thought. Some like Lionel Johnson or Standish O'Grady had achieved a modest immortality without Yeats's help; others like Maud Gonne, George Pollexfen, Thomas Horton or Florence Farr would hardly otherwise be still remembered. To explore these relationships as manifested in his work is to glimpse the man and the poet within a series of more intimate perspectives.

Maud Gonne and the Sorrow of Love

Yeats, as we have seen, met Maud Gonne in 1889, at his father's house in London and was immediately in love. He was conscious of 'a great generosity and courage and a mind without rest', of a complexion that was 'luminous, like that of apple-blossom through which the light falls'.[57] Despite many proposals of marriage, stretching almost through twenty years, she remained unattainable, thereby provoking perhaps the greatest body of love poetry to be written by a modern poet. Between his meeting with her and his marriage in 1917 Yeats had two significant love affairs, with Olivia Shakespear – 'Diana Vernon' – in 1896 and with Florence Farr Emery around 1903. While both these women figure in his poetry and correspondence it is Maud who dominates his poetic imagination through four decades to the very end of his days.

His immediate response to her personality is two-fold: he longs for her in the traditional idiom of unrequited love and

perhaps as a defensive manoeuvre, casts her in myth. Both
these attitudes are to survive in various forms through most
of his life. When she rejects his first proposal of marriage in
1891 he responds by portraying her in epic terms, like the
great fatal women of the past, Deirdre and Helen, who 'come
seldom into the world and always for its trouble':[58]

> Who dreamed that beauty passes like a dream?
> For these red lips, with all their mournful pride,
> Mournful that no new wonder may betide,
> Troy passed away in one high funeral gleam,
> And Usna's children died.

There was little disgrace in being refused by a woman fated
to such large and bloody destinies. The effect of such heroic
casting on the lady and her political aspirations can only be
guessed at. Certainly she showed no signs of wishing to shut
off the poetry by gratifying the passion from which it arose.
There were gains on all sides, except perhaps on the side of
history itself. Nor was the urge to mythologise his beloved
mere defensiveness. Her beauty and 'nobleness' seemed to
redeem the fallen world of Irish politics and Anglo-Saxon
materialism. In a great lyric of 1892 'The Sorrow of Love' —
much revised but never in its basic theme — he imagines her
entry to a world bereft of tragic beauty:

> A girl arose that had red mournful lips
> And seemed the greatness of the world in tears,
> Doomed like Odysseus and the labouring ships
> And proud as Priam murdered with his peers;

transfiguring its humanity with the force of her presence:

> Arose, and on the instant clamorous eaves,
> A climbing moon upon an empty sky,
> And all that lamentation of the leaves,
> Could but compose man's image and his cry.

Meanwhile the private poems are full of what he called 'longing and complaint — the cry of the heart against necessity'. In

'When You are Old', 'The White Birds' and 'A Dream of Death', all written within the same year, the theme is of defeated love. Unexpectedly, in the same year of 1892 a cautionary, if not a critical note enters briefly in 'The Two Trees' where the beloved is urged not to gaze 'in the bitter glass' lest her 'tender eyes grow all unkind'. Whether the warning is against vanity, fanaticism or — as Jeffares suggests — abstract thought, the metaphor returns vengefully in 'A Prayer for my Daughter' almost thirty years later when Anne Yeats is warned against the example of Maud and the lure of the 'looking-glass' lest she lose 'natural kindness' and never find a friend.

That his passion for Maud continued to intensify is borne out not only by the suite of love lyrics addressed to her in his next volume, *The Wind Among the Reeds* (1899), poems of fervour and supplication like 'The Lover tells of the Rose in his Heart' and 'The Cap and Bells' but by the troubled tone of his addresses to Olivia Shakespear in 1896 when she had become his mistress — 'The Travail of Passion' and 'He Bids his Beloved be at Peace'. The heavy sensuality of the former is laced with images of suffering — it is probably his most 'decadent' poem in its blend of sex and religion — where their 'hearts endure the scourge, the plaited thorns' and the 'vinegar-heavy sponge' coming to rest amid 'Lilies of death-pale hope, roses of passionate dream'. The latter rehearses in the same hushed tones the 'vanity of Sleep, Hope, Dream, endless Desire' as that luxuriant, pre-Raphaelite hair — emblem of Olivia as apple-blossom is of Maud — falls on his breast 'Drowning love's lonely hour in deep twilight of rest'. Then in a touching lyric 'The Lover Mourns for the Loss of Love' Maud triumphs and the *affaire* expires.

Pale brows, still hands and dim hair,
I had a beautiful friend
And dreamed that the old despair
Would end in love in the end:
She looked in my heart one day

And saw your image was there;

She has gone weeping away.

Though it seems certain that the love affair with Olivia was revived between then and Yeats's marriage, her presence is not discernible again in his poetry until *The Tower*.

While the image of Olivia subsides in the poetry with 'the nobility of defeated things' — as we have seen she remained prominent in his life and correspondence — Maud continued to gather symbolic accretion. She signifies unattainable beauty for wandering Aengus; she is the mystical rose of the alchemists and the political rose of Irish nationalism; as the 'pity-crazed' Countess Cathleen and as the ally of James Connolly she becomes the secular saint of Ireland's poor. With the turn of the century, however, a note of almost autumnal resignation enters Yeats's verse, together with a new realism of diction and idiom. Those critics who identify his new colloquial style as starting with the shock of Maud's marriage in 1903 seem to overlook the first published dates of 'Adam's Curse' and 'The Folly of Being Comforted'. Both poems were written a year before her marriage and both register the pain of love and the stoicism with which its failure must be endured. Well removed from the lush *fin de siècle* cadences of *The Wind Among the Reeds*, the speakers in 'Adam's Curse' acknowledge that poetry, beauty and love can only be achieved with 'much labouring'. The poem's dying fall leaves Yeats and Maud 'As weary-hearted as that hollow moon'. 'The Folly of Being Comforted' enacts its meaning through the living speech of real human relationship:

One that is ever kind said yesterday:
'Your well-belovèd's hair has threads of grey,
And little shadows come about her eyes;
Time can but make it easier to be wise
Though now it seems impossible, and so
All that you need is patience.'

Heart cries, 'No,

I have not a crumb of comfort, not a grain.
Time can but make her beauty over again:
Because of that great nobleness of hers
The fire that stirs about her, when she stirs,
Burns but more clearly. O she had not these ways
When all the wild summer was in her gaze.'

O heart! O heart! if she'd but turn her head,
You'd know the folly of being comforted.

His salvation was in his ability to mythologise: Maud's kingdom was not of this world; with her heroic destiny she could not be expected to bend to the domesticities of a conventional marriage, even to a poet; union with a boozy patriot who at least shared her vision of Ireland's freedom bloodily won made perhaps better sense. In 'No Second Troy' he forgives her all: the 'misery' with which she filled his days; her traffic with ignorant conspirators; the sanguinary incitements of her speeches. And in forgiving her he manages to absolve himself of failure.

What could have made her peaceful with a mind
That nobleness made simple as a fire,
With beauty like a tightened bow, a kind
That is not natural in an age like this,
Being high and solitary and most stern?
Why, what could she have done, being what she is?
Was there another Troy for her to burn?

Beneath and behind these splendid flourishes there was a great deal of human desperation. The sexual frustration from which Olivia had rescued him some years before had returned to torment him. His recurrent fear that the depressive melancholia of the Pollexfens might break through in his blood was aggravated by the tension and trauma of his days. In the *Memoirs* he records:

It was a time of great personal strain and sorrow. Since my mistress had left me, no other woman had come into my life, and for nearly seven years none did. I was tortured by sexual desire and disappointed love. Often as I walked the woods at Coole it would have been a relief to have screamed aloud. When desire became an unendurable torture, I would masturbate, and that, no matter how moderate I was, would make me ill. It never occurred to me to seek another love. I would repeat to myself again and again the last confession of Lancelot, and indeed it was my greatest pride, 'I have loved a queen beyond measure and exceeding long.' I was never before or since so miserable as in those years that followed my first visit to Coole. In the second as during the first visit my nervous system was worn out. The toil of dressing in the morning exhausted me, and Lady Gregory began to send me cups of soup when I was called.[59]

Never having received maternal tenderness from Susan Yeats and having come recently from the house of his gloomy, hypochondriac uncle, George Pollexfen, he found the warmth and sanity of Lady Gregory and her gracious, well-ordered house, a perfect sanctuary from his ills. In the work routine she set him and in the visits she made with him to the neighbouring cottages his creative energies revived and what he was later to call 'the book of the people' opened to his consciousness. One can understand how, on hearing of her illness in February 1909, he wrote: 'She had been to me mother, friend, sister and brother. I cannot realise the world without her — she brought to my wavering thoughts steadfast nobility.'[60]

His sexual loneliness, however, needed more specific comfort and this came in the form of Florence Farr Emery. Her personality — which will come up again in connection with 'All Souls Night' — was marked by its vitality, naturalness and daring. Yeats met her first in 1890 when she was performing in John Todhunter's 'Sicilian Idyll' at Bedford Park. She was Shaw's mistress for a period in the 1890s and played in the first production of *Arms and the Man* which was put on in London with Yeats's *Land of Heart's Desire* as a curtain raiser. As we have noted she came to Dublin and played Aleel in the first production of *The Countess Cathleen* (1899). Shaw wrote that she 'set no bounds to her relations with men whom she liked' and that she was 'in violent reaction against Victorian morals, especially sexual and domestic morals'.[61] The editor of Yeats's and Shaw's letters to her, Clifford Bax, recalled her 'starry eyes' and declared her 'one of the four or five genuinely poetic women whom I have known'.[62]

Shaw records that he and Florence 'detached ourselves from one another naturally and painlessly; and presently I got married' and that she 'found the friend she really needed in Yeats'. With Yeats she practised 'cantillating', reciting poetry to the harp or psaltery and they gave a series of performances through England. His letters to her, beginning early in 1903, reveal a humorous, zestful, rather than a passionate relationship. He contemplates a cycling trip to Canterbury — he is 'fired by Chaucer' — 'with some harmless person to keep up appearances.' He joins in her 'eastern meditation' aiming at some 'dynamic and substantialising force as distinguished from the eastern quiescent and supersensualizing state of soul — a movement downwards upon life not upwards out of life'. Contemplating a visit to her in London in 1906 he writes of the 'pleasure it is to be fond of somebody to whom I can talk — as a rule any sort of affection annihilates conversation'.

> To be moved and talkative, unrestrained, one's own self, and to be this not because one has created some absurd delusion that it is all wisdom ... this is the best in life. All this means that I am looking forward to seeing you — that my spirits rise at the thought of it.[63]

Her companionship was the perfect anodyne for his guilt-ridden sexual need and nervous depression. She was the only woman, he later confided in his wife, 'to whom I could tell *everything*.' The affair ended because 'she got bored'. She went to Ceylon in 1912 as 'Lady Superintendent' of a Buddhist college where she died of cancer in 1917. She corresponded with Yeats to the end and her spirit is summoned in the great meditation of 'All Souls' Night'.

Maud Gonne continued to dominate his thought: her

inspiration has already yielded a variety of moods to his poetry:
in the lyrics of 'longing and complaint' she appeared as the
traditional 'Belle Dame sans Merci', then as epic heroine,
symbol of resurgent Ireland and wife of MacBride who must
be elaborately and ingeniously absolved of cruelty and bad
faith. After the break up of the marriage and after Yeats had
extricated himself from what Hone described as 'a liaison with
an unmarried woman past her first youth' the image of Maud
made a powerful return to his poetic imagination. The over-
riding theme of the new poems she inspired is memory, the
mood one of excited nostalgia for her beauty and magnanimity. For the first time he seemed able to contemplate without
irritation and jealousy her service to the people and more
particularly to the poor. The time was 1915-16, the poems
are 'Memory', 'Her Praise', 'The People', 'His Phoenix', 'A
Thought from Propertius', 'Broken Dreams', 'A Deep-sworn
Vow' and 'Presences'. These great poems have transcended the
languour and the shrillness of his early love lyrics and they
reveal an advance, in terms of maturity and realism, even on
'Adam's Curse'.

In a remarkable feat of 'impersonality' the poet manages
to keep his own possessiveness and pain in check while
focussing with passionate objectivity upon the beloved.

> There is grey in your hair.
> Young men no longer suddenly catch their breath
> When you are passing;
> But maybe some old gaffer mutters a blessing
> Because it was your prayer
> Recovered him from the bed of death.
> For your sole sake — that all heart's ache have known,
> And given to others all heart's ache,
> From meagre girlhood's putting on
> Burdensome beauty — for your sole sake
> Heaven has put away the stroke of her doom,
> So great her portion in that peace you make
> By merely walking in a room.

Most love poetry is the projection of the poet's personality upon the love object. The greatness of these lines is in their compassionate sense of the whole person, girl and woman, private and public self. In 'The People', Yeats, with an admittedly rare humility, appoints Maud his 'phoenix', as his mentor and example in the conduct of his human transactions.

As the poem opens Yeats 'sets himself up' — rather in the manner of 'Easter 1916' — inveighing against the 'daily spite of this unmannerly town' where 'who has served the most is most defamed'. Invoking his nascent theory of history he longs for a world like Renaissance Italy where in his proper 'phase' he might have walked

> In the green shadow of Ferrara wall;
> Or climbed among the images of the past —
> The unperturbed and courtly images —
> Evening and morning, the steep street of Urbino
> To where the Duchess and her people talked
> The stately midnight through. . . .

He might, he complains, 'have used the one substantial right / My trade allows: chosen my company'. Maud's reply shows a side of her nature we have not seen before in the poetry, nor elsewhere in the commentary her life has provoked.

> Thereon my phoenix answered in reproof,
> 'The drunkards, pilferers of public funds,
> All the dishonest crowd I had driven away,
> When my luck changed and they dared meet my face,
> Crawled from obscurity, and set upon me
> Those I had served and some that I had fed;
> Yet never have I, now nor any time,
> Complained of the people.'

The poet's answer to her reproof — 'After nine years, I sink my head abashed' — suggests not only a calming of the erotic ego but a possible revival of his hopes for marriage. Since his affair with the 'woman past her first youth' Lady Gregory had been urging him to settle down. He had been making

devious poetic overtures to the maturing Iseult in poems like
'To a Child Dancing in the Wind' and its sequel. As he braced
himself for his last proposal to Maud and having hedged his
bets a little with her daughter, a dream like this in 'Presences'
comes as if 'the hair stood up on my head'.

> They stood in the door and stood between
> My great wood lectern and the fire
> Till I could hear their hearts beating:
> One is a harlot, and one a child
> That never looked upon man with desire,
> And one, it may be, a queen.

The outcome of his embassy to Maud and Iseult we know. In
the years following his marriage Maud is virtually banished
from his poetry and when she is readmitted it is with much
diminished status. Whether Yeats is smarting from his final
rejection, or on the other hand determined to reassure his new
bride that the past is behind him, his Phoenix pursues a rather
wraith-like course through *Michael Robartes and the Dancer,
The Tower, The Winding Stair* and *A Full Moon in March*. She
is remembered for 'her opinionated mind' in 'A Prayer for My
Daughter' and in 'Among School Children' as a daughter of
the swan changed by time to a creature 'Hollow of cheek
as though it drank the wind / And took a mess of shadows for
its meat'. Again she is permitted to mingle anonymously with
the many ladies, real and fabulous, that make up the cast of
the companion poems, 'A Man Young and Old' and 'A Woman
Young and Old'. Then in the *Last Poems* she makes her
triumphant return.

Here the setting for her is the Yeatsian apocalypse, the
grand implosion of the gyre, the consummation which Maud
had mysteriously foreshadowed in the early lyrics when 'Troy
passed away in one high funeral gleam / And Usna's children
died'. Now against a background of mounting barbarism and
human degeneration her majestic presence is invoked as a last
'counter truth' to pose against the levelling spirit of the age.
First we see her in 'Beautiful Lofty Things', where Yeats

assembles five personages to epitomise his idea of embodied human grandeur. As we shall be glancing at some of the other characters in it I quote the poem in full.

> Beautiful lofty things: O'Leary's noble head;
> My father upon the Abbey stage, before him a raging crowd:
> 'This Land of Saints,' and then as the applause died out,
> 'Of plaster Saints'; his beautiful mischievous head thrown
> > back.
> Standish O'Grady supporting himself between the tables
> Speaking to a drunken audience high nonsensical words;
> Augusta Gregory seated at her great ormolu table,
> Her eightieth winter approaching: 'Yesterday he threatened
> > my life.
> I told him that nightly from six to seven I sat at this table,
> The blinds drawn up'; Maud Gonne at Howth station
> > waiting a train,
> Pallas Athene in that straight back and arrogant head:
> All the Olympians; a thing never known again.

Having placed Maud on the throne of Olympus — she certainly is granted the strongest position in the poem — Yeats, as I have argued elsewhere,[64] evokes her as first among the 'hound voices' of his strange, threatening poem of 1938, 'Hound Voice' where he sees an elite *corps* of warrior spirits holding the line in some Irish Armageddon:

> The women that I picked spoke sweet and low
> And yet gave tongue. 'Hound Voices' were they all.
> We picked each other from afar and knew
> What hour of terror comes to test the soul,
> And in that terror's name obeyed the call. . . .

But her apotheoisis is in 'A Bronze Head'. In the first two stanzas he contemplates Lawrence Campbell's sculpture of Maud near the entrance to the Municipal Gallery — 'Human, superhuman, a bird's round eye' — recapitulating his early praise of her gentleness and 'magnanimity'. Then in a startling third stanza he sees her early self as having the grace and mettle of a thoroughbred race-horse, with its natural force and

headlong, predestined course:

> But even at the starting-post, all sleek and new,
> I saw the wildness in her, and I thought
> A vision of terror that it must live through
> Had shattered her soul. Propinquity had brought
> Imagination to that pitch where it casts out
> All that is not itself: I had grown wild
> And wandered murmuring everywhere, 'My child, my child'.

From this compassionate vision of a young woman, vulnerably beautiful, Yeats turns to the goddess figure, 'daughter of the swan', looking out upon a fallen political world from her 'bird's round eye'.

> Or else I thought her supernatural;
> As though a sterner eye looked through her eye
> On this foul world in its decline and fall;
> On gangling stocks grown great, great stocks run dry,
> Ancestral pearls all pitched into a sty,
> Heroic reverie mocked by clown and knave,
> And wondered what was left for massacre to save.

It is clear that his love and admiration for her not only survived the pain and attrition of the years, but grew in breadth and intensity to the end. Her 'pilgrim soul' rules his imagination from her 'first putting on burdensome beauty', it epitomises the pity, the sorrow and finally the terror of love and triumphs in the end as his type for human excellence and tragic muse of history.

Lionel Johnson, John Synge, George Pollexfen, W. T. Horton, Florence Emery, MacGregor Mathers

'In Memory of Major Robert Gregory' and 'All Souls Night', separated by two years, adopt the form of the 'conversation poem' which Yeats developed from Coleridge's example in 'Dejection', 'Frost at Midnight' and 'This Lime Tree Bower my Prison'. The form assumes a definite scene and decor —

mostly the poet's room — and a continuous reverie in the present tense in which the poet's voice is overheard communing with itself and with absent friends. The meditation and the choice of friends may, usually does, pretend a randomness, a sense of mental drift which is sometimes at odds with its formal symmetry. Its great advantage is its opportunity to create atmosphere, to invoke a sense of stillness and immediacy, to follow the curve of memory and to end when the mood seems to subside. Thus spontaneity is achieved by ingenious artifice. [117]

The opening stanzas of 'Major Robert Gregory' record with satisfaction that the poet and George have settled into their house, the tower, and that their hospitality, this night, must be reserved for dead friends. There is, perhaps, a touch of stoicism in the suggestion that some living friends of the poet might not yet be entirely welcome to his wife.

> Always we'd have the new friends meet the old
> And we are hurt if either friend seem cold,
> And there is salt to lengthen out the smart
> In the affections of our heart,
> And quarrels are blown up upon that head.

Clearly it is not yet time to ask the Widow MacBride. But the occasion is auspicious for a review of past friendships — Lionel Johnson, John Synge, George Pollexfen and the prime subject of the poem, the dead airman, Robert Gregory.

> Lionel Johnson comes the first to mind,
> Who loved his learning better than mankind,
> Though courteous to the worst; much falling he
> Brooded upon sanctity
> Till all his Greek and Latin learning seemed
> A long blast upon the horn that brought
> A little nearer to his thought
> A measureless consummation that he dreamed.

Lionel Johnson, Catholic poet and one of Yeats's 'tavern comrades' of the *Cheshire Cheese* in the 1890s is recalled for three traits which, though alien to Yeats, filled him with curiosity. Classical learning, Christian sanctity and the illumination of 'the wine-vat' were approaches towards vision, insight or wisdom that he observed and celebrated in others throughout his life: in 'The Seven Sages', for instance, he rejects the mind that never 'looked out of the eye of a saint', or 'out of a drunkard's eye.' In 'The Tragic Generation' he recalls Johnson's behaviour with especial vividness: 'he rose from his stair, took a step towards me in his eagerness, and fell on to the floor; and I saw that he was drunk.' Though the phrase 'much falling' may refer to this incident and to the fact that Johnson died in a fall from a bar-stool — as critics never tire of pointing out — it takes in a much larger world of Christian sin and repentance, together with a mysterious sense of evil which Yeats described as 'psychological depths I could never enter': 'Did the austerity, the melancholy of his thoughts, that spiritual ecstasy which he touched at times, heighten, as complementary colours heighten one another, not only the Vision of Evil, but its fascination?'

It was natural that Yeats would feel the lure of Catholicism in that era when it was such a cult among the decadent aesthetes — Stenbock and the Beardsleys, Dowson and Johnson, Francis Thomson, eventually even Wilde. His affection for Christianity never faded: one of his most beguiling letters describes in later years his wife, George, teaching Michael the Lord's Prayer in the sitting-room at Ballylee. The temptation to become 'a Christian man' himself, however, is finally and firmly laid aside in the poem 'Vacillation' (1933) where he mildly dismisses Von Hugel with 'blessings on his head' and makes his own robust act of faith: 'Homer is my example and his unchristened heart'. Synge is Johnson's antithesis:

And that enquiring man John Synge comes next,
That dying chose the living world for text
And never could have rested in the tomb
But that, long travelling, he had come

Towards nightfall upon certain set apart
In a most desolate stony place,
Towards nightfall upon a race
Passionate and simple like his heart.

Instead of book learning Synge studied 'mankind' in its direct, primitive manifestation. Like Johnson and Yeats himself his life had been a search for truth. Again the path he chose and towards which he had been directed by Yeats had brought him to his special vision, 'to where passion, living through its thousand purgatorial years, as in the wink of an eye, becomes wisdom'.[65] Johnson had said to Yeats: 'You need ten years in a library, but I have need of ten years in the wilderness.' It was part of Yeats's genius that he lived somewhere in between, observing with tireless vigilance the choices of others:

And then I think of old George Pollexfen,
In muscular youth well known to Mayo men
For horsemanship at meets or at racecourses,
That could have shown how pure-bred horses
And solid men, for all their passion, live
But as the outrageous stars incline
By opposition, square and trine;
Having grown sluggish and contemplative.

The figure of George Pollexfen is complicated by that kinship which Yeats regarded with a blend of pride and fear: pride that it had not passed through any 'huckster's loin' and fear of the depressive melancholia that it carried in its genes. Thematically George Pollexfen rounds out the psychological pattern, being a man divided between the elemental instinct for horseflesh and the astrologer's recourse to the outrageous stars for guidance. Yeats had stayed with him at his house at Thornhill, Sligo when a youth and had shared visions with him and his clairvoyant servant, Mary Battle. More significantly, perhaps, he had stayed with him for six months during the 'most miserable time' of his life when he had parted with Olivia Shakespear and suffered those

extremities of sexual frustration we have already seen. This
[120] helps to explain his presence in a poem otherwise devoted to
young men, Yeats's contemporaries, who had died untimely.
There is, I suspect, a final reason: the mystery of a man who
never explained himself, a quality which Yeats admired in
Synge and envied in Maud Gonne – 'You, that have not lived
in thought but deed, / Can have the purity of a natural force.'
It is the dominating virtue of Robert Gregory, towards whom
the meditation is moving and it was a hall mark of the
Pollexfen temperament. Yeats recalled with delight old
William decapitating an egg with one knife-stroke, indifferent
as to where the top went and, with a mixture of resentment
and respect, the fact that 'if there was but one kidney with
the bacon at breakfast he [George] always took it without
apology.' John B. Yeats who had been at school with
George had found him full of strange 'magnetism' and an
example of 'the awesome helplessness of ultimate human
nature'.[66]

Therefore when we turn to Robert Gregory, whose memory
occupies the second half of the poem, elaborate co-ordinates
of judgment on life and death have been established. We have
already seen how Yeats cherished Gregory's personality for
its Renaissance *sprezzatura*, that effortless style that encom-
passes so many gifts. Now when we turn towards Gregory, to
the sweep and energy of his career as soldier, scholar, horseman, painter, writer, landlord, fighter-pilot, the self-absorbed,
specialist obsessions of the poet's three 'close companions'
are somehow diminished. Only Gregory seems to be fully and
victoriously human. Even his 'scholarship' appears as that of
one who lives 'not in thought but deed', who has therefore
the 'purity of a natural force'. The poem's transition reminds
us of the sedentary poet envying the fighting men in 'The
Road to my Door', or calling to the spirit of Cuchulain in
'Ego Dominus Tuus', or most particularly the end of 'Among
School Children' where he turns from blear-eyed philosophers
and contemplative nuns to the 'great rooted blossomer' and
the dancer's 'body swayed to music'.

In such a poem as 'The Choice', Yeats had deliberated between 'Perfection of the life, or of the work'. Johnson and [121] Synge had striven for the work. George Pollexfen with his unreflective 'awesome helplessness' had fumbled between the two. The verve and perfection of Gregory's life was canonised in his violent death, making the life, ironically, a perfect work of art, enforcing the tragic proverb that those whom the gods love die young.

> Some burn damp faggots, others may consume
> The entire combustible world in one small room
> As though dried straw, and if we turn about
> The bare chimney is gone black out
> Because the work had finished in that flare.
> Soldier, scholar, horseman, he,
> As 'twere all life's epitome.
> What made us dream that he could comb grey hair?

It is at this moment of definition that Yeats begins to turn down the volume of his reverie. He had intended to have 'brought to mind' so many others 'that manhood tried, or childhood loved' but he cannot go on because 'that late death took all my heart for speech'. Though the stanzas on Gregory are distinguished by their clarity of detail, energy of movement and daylight colour, their effect is dramatically one of mystery. The 'lonely impulse' of Gregory's life is the more astonishing and inscrutable for having been lived in terms of plain, visible action.

'All Souls' Night' was, as we have seen, written at Oxford in November 1920. In his dedication of *A Vision* – the poem was appended as a coda to its first edition – he recalls his sense of triumph at finding in the automatic script so many answers to the mysteries of the soul, history and human personality. These answers had come to him unsought 'when I had ceased all active search, yet had not ceased from desire'. Now he has shaped them into a coherent system which is 'the first to substitute for Biblical or mythological figures, historical movements and actual men and women'. He goes on:

'I have moments of exaltation like that in which I wrote "All [122] Souls' Night", but I have other moments when remembering my ignorance of philosophy I doubt if I can make another share my excitement.'

But the ghosts of his contemplative friends will understand. He therefore sets out, in best spiritualist hospitality, 'two long glasses brimmed with muscatel' — spirits drink of the 'wine-breath' unlike 'our gross palates' which 'drink from the whole wine' — because he has 'a marvellous thing to say'. He then calls up in turn Horton, Florence Emery and MacGregor Mathers to share his reverie.

> Horton's the first I call. He loved strange thought
> And knew that sweet extremity of pride
> That's called platonic love,
> And that to such a pitch of passion wrought
> Nothing could bring him, when his lady died,
> Anodyne for his love.
> Words were but wasted breath;
> One dear hope had he:
> The inclemency
> Of that or the next winter would be death.

Horton's presence here has puzzled critics; even more surprise is evinced at Yeats's wish to have dedicated *A Vision* to him had he lived. Before going into the biographical relation between the two men, one can immediately see a poetic reason for his inclusion side by side with Florence Emery. As in 'Major Robert Gregory', opposite is counterposed to opposite: Horton's austere platonic love to her gleeful sexuality: his Christian asceticism which made him in the end a Catholic, her eastern mysticism that led her to Ceylon. The story of Horton, however, is more complex and has been admirably set out in George Mills Harper's *Record of an Occult Friendship*. Relevant to our purpose is the fact that W. T. Horton was initiated by Yeats into the Golden Dawn in that momentous year of 1896, that he left it because of its anti-Christian bias and hounded Yeats for his continued membership of it till he died in 1919, a year before the poem was written. His attacks were perhaps the most personally wounding of all that Yeats received, yet it was through the poet's patience and humility that the strange and valuable friendship survived: attacks like this, written in 1914:

> To see you on the floor among those papers searching for an automatic script, where one man finds a misquotation among them, while round you sit your guests, shocked me for it stood out as a terrible symbol. I saw you as the man with the muck rake in '*The Pilgrim's Progress*' while above you your Beloved held the dazzling crown of your own Poetic Genius. But you would not look up and went on with your grovelling.[67]

Horton saw visions, among them one urgently relevant to Yeats, the image of his soul being drawn between a dark and a white horse. He exhorts Yeats to 'give the dark horse wings & subordinate it to the white winged horse' or risk disaster. Among the first of George Yeats's automatic scripts three years later was a reference to these black and white winged horses. Yeats, whose theme in *A Vision* was 'The Way of the Soul between the Sun and the Moon', insisted on favouring the dark horse which he associated with the passionate or lunar side of destiny. When he consulted his Instructors through George after Horton's death, however, he was relieved to learn that his cautionary friend 'believes now much that he denied before, he says you are right, he says he is so happy that he weeps'.

Yeats, therefore, had from Horton the best of both worlds: his antinomial horses provided the deep structure of *A Vision*, yet Yeats's contrary reading of the symbols proved not only right but was sealed with the *imprimatur* of his friend's spirit. The thought throws complex light on Horton's earthly love for his lady, Amy Locke, who had died in 1916.

> Two thoughts were so mixed up I could not tell
> Whether of her or God he thought the most,
> But think that his mind's eye,

When upward turned, on one sole image fell;
And that a slight companionable ghost
Wild with divinity,
Had so lit up the whole
Immense miraculous house
The Bible promised us,
It seemed a gold-fish swimming in a bowl.

Horton's beatific vision, the beloved's 'wild' divinity and the homely yet sensual image of the gold-fish bowl, seems mildly to rebuke the self-denial of his earthly choices.

Horton had turned from an amorous life to one of celibacy; Florence Emery from an amorous life to one of oriental meditation. Before she left for Ceylon she seems to have been told she had cancer, a fact ignored by Yeats unless his reference to her 'first wrinkles' and 'foul years' are a euphemism for it. He ignores their love affair, perhaps out of delicacy, more probably because her role in the poem, like that of Horton and MacGregor, is to dramatise the quest for the soul's way between the sun and the moon.

Before that end much had she ravelled out
From a discourse in figurative speech
By some learned Indian
On the soul's journey. How it is whirled about,
Wherever the orbit of the moon can reach,
Until it plunge into the sun;
And there, free and yet fast,
Being both Chance and Choice,
Forget its broken toys
And sink into its own delight at last.

MacGregor's role in Yeats's life has already been glanced at and we are not surprised to see his formidable ghost come forward to complete the *dramatis personae*. The evocation is magnificent, imbued with all the swagger and force of its subject.

And I call up MacGregor from the grave,
For in my first hard springtime we were friends,

> Although of late estranged.
> I thought him half a lunatic, half knave,
> And told him so, but friendship never ends;
> And what if mind seem changed,
> And it seem changed with the mind
> When thoughts rise up unbid
> On generous things that he did
> And I grow half contented to be blind!

The Wordsworthian echo of 'hard springtime' enforces the central theme of the soul's growth, and in poetic terms gives MacGregor pride of place among the poet's spiritual exemplars. On the other hand the vacillation of the language — 'although', 'but', 'what if', the recurrence of 'half' — and his placing in the poem suggest a tragic inadequacy like that of George Pollexfen in 'Major Robert Gregory'. As MacGregor's portrait is rounded out the poem swings back to Yeats in his Oxford study, the 'living man' who of all these intrepid 'discoverers of forgotten truth' survives to write the poems.

> He had much industry in setting out,
> Much boistrous courage, before loneliness
> Had driven him crazed;
> For meditations upon unknown thought
> Make human intercourse grow less and less;
> They are neither paid nor praised.
> But he'd object to the host,
> The glass because my glass;
> A ghost-lover he was
> And may have grown more arrogant being a ghost.

Yeats's 'moment of exaltation' in the poem, his 'marvellous thing' to say, to the disappointment of some critics, never actually gets said in the text. It is, of course, eloquently implicit. On the night of All Souls 1920 he has found the answer they had all been searching for and despite the obstacles and pit-falls has preserved his health and sanity to promulgate it in prose and verse.

Both poems are bedded in this world, in marital happiness and domestic calm, but above all in the strength of poetic authority. His occult intimations had always brought him [126] 'metaphors for poetry'. There is a distinct note of self-gratulation in both poems, especially the second. But it is redeemed by the generosity of his concern for his dead friends — Johnson, Synge, Pollexfen, Gregory, Horton, Florence and MacGregor — who now drink of the wine-breath while their earthly celebrant drinks of the full wine and rejoices in the bridgehead he has won between their two worlds.

> Such thought — such thought have I that hold it tight
> Till meditations master all its parts,
> Nothing can stay my glance
> Until that glance run in the world's despite
> To where the damned have howled away their hearts,
> And where the blessed dance;
> Such thought, that in it bound
> I need no other thing,
> Wound in mind's wandering
> As mummies in the mummy-cloth are wound.

Mabel Beardsley

Our last great poem celebrating a human relationship is Yeats's longest poem in the vein, 'Upon a Dying Lady', which monitors the final illness and impending death of the actress Mabel Beardsley. The event was vividly documented in two letters to Lady Gregory in January and February of 1913. In the first Yeats reports: 'Strange that just after writing those lines on the Rhymers who 'unrepenting faced their ends' I should be at the bedside of the dying sister of Beardsley, who was practically one of us.' He describes how the painter Ricketts had brought in four dolls 'dressed like people out of her brother's drawings ... Women with loose trousers and boys that looked like women'. Yeats tells Mabel of Florence Emery's life in Ceylon to which she replies: 'How fine for her, but a girls' school! Why she used to make even me blush!' and continues to entertain her visitors with 'improper stories'. He is struck by her courage, 'her strange charm — the pathetic gaiety.' Clearly she is the female as Gregory is the male version of *sprezzatura*:

> She had all the great lady airs and asked after my work and my health as if they were the most important things in the world to her. 'A palmist told me,' she said, 'that when I was forty-two my life would take a turn for the better and now I shall spend my forty-second year in heaven' and then emphatically 'O yes I shall go to heaven. Papists do.'

Yeats was good at visiting the sick. By his second letter an intimacy had grown between them: 'I always see her alone now. She keeps Sunday afternoon for me.' The lyric sequence which these visits inspired is unique among Yeats's poems for its concern with characterisation: with a series of minute strokes he builds her personality through description, dialogue and action. Few writers of fiction have achieved such precision and intensity, such particularity of place and atmosphere and such felt human life within so small a compass:

> With the old kindness, the old distinguished grace,
> She lies, her lovely piteous head amid dull red hair
> Propped upon pillows, rouge on the pallor of her face.
> She would not have us sad because she is lying there,
> And when she meets our gaze her eyes are laughter-lit,
> Her speech a wicked tale that we may vie with her,
> Matching our broken-hearted wit against her wit,
> Thinking of saints and of Petronius Arbiter.

The balance between Christian sainthood and pagan extravagance, — we may recall that Petronius was Nero's *arbiter elegantiae* — between the demands of her religion and the outrageous art of her brother and his associates, is finely maintained as the poem moves through its seven lyrics. The second describes the dolls that surround her, concluding

> We have given the world our passion,
> We have naught for death but toys.

The third describes the stolid priest's entry upon this theatre
of contradictions:

> Because to-day is some religious festival
> They had a priest say Mass, and even the Japanese,
> Heel up and weight on toe, must face the wall
> — Pedant in passion, learned in old courtesies,
> Vehement and witty she had seemed —; the Venetian lady
> Who had seemed to glide to some intrigue in her red shoes
> Her domino, her pannieried skirt copied from Longhi;
> The meditative critic; all are on their toes,
> Even our Beauty with her Turkish trousers on.
> Because the priest must have like every dog his day
> Or keep us all awake with baying at the moon,
> We and our dolls being but the world were best away.

The fourth movement exploits the mutiple ironies of the 'play'
in which the dying actress is absorbed: she is a child playing
with life's toys; an actress cast centrally in a play; for both
the interruption of the play 'half done' is intolerable. But the
death scene is real as 'fantastical and wild' she plays it out
before her last audience. It is therefore in the fifth movement,
'Her Race', that Yeats's sense of her true aristocracy comes
into living definition. The Beardsleys are in conventional terms
lower middle class, but with 'her dead brother's valour' Mabel
transcends the incivility and commonness of 'narrow natures'
as she faces death without faltering in the style which had
distinguished her life and art. Thus the apprehension of her
going forces Yeats into a declaration of confused sympathy
with her Papist faith in the afterlife.

> When her soul flies to the predestined dancing-place
> (I have no speech but symbol, the pagan speech I made
> Amid the dreams of youth) let her come face to face,
> Amid that first astonishment, with Grania's shade,
> All but the terrors of the woodland flight forgot
> That made her Diarmuid dear, and some old cardinal
> Pacing with half-closed eyelids in a sunny spot
> Who had murmured of Giorgione at his latest breath —

Aye, and Achilles, Timor, Babar, Barhaim, all
Who have lived in joy and laughed into the face of Death.   [129]

The poet's headlong swerves between Tir na nOg, Elysium, the Mongol and Islamic heavens and an acceptable Catholic version of paradise are, perhaps, the most touching evidence of how deeply the experience has moved him.

The poem ends with a poignant apostrophe to death, 'pardon, great enemy' — Yeats is currently digesting Grierson's edition of Donne published the previous year (1912) — as her friends bring into the deathroom their Christmas tree hung with 'pretty things' to please 'a fantastic head':

Give her a little grace,
What if a laughing eye
Have looked into your face?
It is about to die.

'Upon a Dying Lady' is among the most human of Yeats's poems. In its wit and tenderness and in the intricate ironies of its elegiac mood, in its vivid, particular sense of another's existential being, it has no counterpart in Yeats and few in modern literature. Certainly it gives the lie to those who would characterise Yeats as lacking in compassion or in an awareness of people outside himself. It is the most gravely intimate of all his reveries on friendship.

The last word on Mabel Beardsley and on that vivid, wilful Edwardian era whose spirit she embodied is best left to Florence Farr, herself one of its last and most engaging exemplars. Here is how George Yeats brings both together in her preface to her husband's letters to Florence.

In January 1917 she had an operation and writes in pencil 'When I found a report was being spread that I had a *boil*, I was most indignant at being supposed to have such a nasty disease. Cancer seems decent and dry. It is quite an experience for me as I have never been helpless in my life since I was a baby.' She is gay and courageous about it all. Did she remember, I wonder, that she had written two years earlier to WBY on hearing from him that Mabel Beardsley was dying of cancer, 'I am always glad to hear of someone making a brave end. I came here to make mine brave and I seem to have started another incarnation.'

Throughout the *Last Poems* the roll call of proper names goes on: Caesar, Helen and Michael Angelo conspire to create the meaning of 'The Long-legged Fly'; John Bull is apostrophised on behalf of Roger Casement; 'Calvert and Wilson, Blake and Claude' are cited as visionary witnesses; relatives like William Pollexfen and 'the smuggler Middleton' are remembered; semi-fabulous characters like Colonel Martin or John Kinsella point a moral or adorn a tale. In the midst of these presences there remain the prized personal relationships which still gather to themselves a unique aura in the poetry. The principle of their inclusion seems to involve a special poetic empathy on the poet's apprehension of their character. Thus Dorothy Wellesley, intimate friend of his declining years, inspires a rich mysterious lyric, while Ethel Mannin who figures as prominently in the correspondence, gains no foothold on the verse. Margot Ruddock, despite her madness and the trouble she had caused him, is remembered in two plaintive lyrics and admitted to the company of 'beautiful lofty things'. It is this same sense of poetry, of the 'wasteful virtues' that determines the choice in 'Beautiful Lofty Things' which has already been quoted in full.

Looking back on his lifetime Yeats chooses, or is chosen by, five haunting moments, each epitomised by an image of a friend caught in a defining posture. Readers of the poetry will have little difficulty in seeing why four of these moments and persons are saluted in such honorific terms: 'O'Leary's noble head', the 'beautiful mischievous head' of John B. Yeats facing the Abbey riot; Lady Gregory defying the assassin's threat; Maud Gonne at Howth Station. This setting for Maud stresses the fact that no especial moment in history is envisaged for each. The vision is private, a remarkable human presence transcending a mundane context.

Standish James O'Grady however is making his first appearance, at a very late stage, in Yeats's poetry. There are several objective reasons, of course, why O'Grady should be remembered in the context: because of his *History of Ireland* and heroic prose romances he had merited from A.E. the title 'Father of the Literary Revival'; as a 'Fenian Unionist' he had called upon the Irish landlords to resume the leadership of the Irish people. He had indeed foretold the course of Irish history in the speech Yeats refers to in the poem, speaking of a literary, then a political movement and: 'then must come a military movement, that will be important indeed.' Unlike the Abbey crowd this 'drunken audience' applauds, 'understanding nothing but the sweetness of the voice, the nobility of the gesture.'[68] That is obviously the moment when O'Grady, looking out of a 'drunkard's eye' transcends his occasion and achieves beauty and loftiness. It is that gesture of 'sprezzatura' that places him with O'Leary and the poet's father among the Olympians.

With the two ladies the poem becomes quieter and more private – 'The women that I picked spoke sweet and low / And yet gave tongue' – Lady Gregory 'sitting at her great ormolu table' disdaining the threat to her life, and finally Maud at Howth station. This moment is emphatically private. On an evening in July 1891 Yeats had proposed marriage to Maud in her room at the Nassau Hotel, Dublin and had been reluctantly, soulfully refused: 'but in words that had no conventional ring she asked for my friendship.' They spent the following day at Howth, dining with her old nurse whom Yeats overheard asking if they 'were engaged to be married.'[69] Of all his Olympians Maud might most easily have been placed before 'a raging crowd' where her distinction would have had public vindication. But that is not the kind of immortality he is conferring. The pantheon arises out of intimate personal feeling and is validated alone by the authority of poetic vision. As in the case of a later Irish poet, Patrick Kavanagh, 'Gods make their own importance.'

'The Municipal Gallery Revisited' is our final example of

Yeats's poetic dialogue with his *milieu*, as its thought moves
inward from the array of public figures, friends and acquaintances depicted on the canvasses, to the unique status of Synge
and Lady Gregory. He ponders, first casually, 'the images of
thirty years' –

> Casement upon trial, half hidden by the bars,
> Guarded; Griffith staring in hysterical pride;
> Kevin O'Higgins' countenance that wears
> A gentle questioning look that cannot hide
> A soul incapable of remorse or rest;
> A revolutionary soldier kneeling to be blessed.

He moves – as through that long schoolroom in 'Among
School Children' – noting among the 'permanent and
impermanent images' the toll death has taken of his friends:
'Augusta Gregory's son; her sister's son, / Hugh Lane, "onlie
begetter" of all these', until he comes to Mancini's portrait
of Lady Gregory herself:

> 'Greatest since Rembrandt', according to John Synge;
> A great ebullient portrait certainly;
> But where is the brush that could show anything
> Of all that pride and that humility?

From this point on the presences of his two dead friends
invade the poem, just as Robert Gregory had taken over the
second half of his elegy. After the picture of Lady Gregory
and before the picture of 'John Synge himself' Yeats defines
their life-giving ministry to the 'dead Ireland of my youth'
mentioned in the second stanza:

> John Synge, I and Augusta Gregory, thought
> All that we did, all that we said or sang
> Must come from contact with the soil, from that
> Contact everything Antaeus-like grew strong.
> We three alone in modern times had brought
> Everything down to that sole test again,
> Dream of the noble and the beggar-man.

In the next and final stanza Yeats stands before his father's portrait of John Synge, 'that rooted man'. Here, as Helen [133] Vendler has pointed out in a brilliant insight, much that was latent in the poem now becomes explicit:

> We have seen Augusta Gregory, we now see John Synge. Between them, if the gallery and the elegy are to coincide, should hang one other portrait – the portrait, we realize, that this whole poem, in another medium, has been drawing – the self-portrait of William Butler Yeats. And immediately that effigy is before us, and we, his readers, have replaced the poet as the gazers in the gallery.[70]

Thus he asks not just to be memorialized in a picture, or merely to be remembered by his books, but to survive in the context of those creative friendships which had shaped the fabric of his life and art:

> You that would judge me, do not judge alone
> This book or that, come to this hallowed place
> Where my friends' portraits hang and look thereon;
> Ireland's history in their lineaments trace;
> Think where man's glory most begins and ends,
> And say my glory was I had such friends.

References

In such a short book I thought it best not to have too fussy a proliferation of footnote references through the text, especially as so many of the key quotations come from a small number of recurrent and recognisable sources – the collected poems, plays and fictions, the *Autobiographies* and *Memoirs*, the letters and the various volumes of his collected essays and reviews. Therefore no quotations from Yeats's poetry and drama are footnoted where the name of the poem or play is given in the text. When his correspondence is cited the reference will be to Wade's great edition of the *Letters* unless otherwise indicated. In regard to the letters and the other volumes of primary sources all the more substantial quotations are referenced. Where a short phrase is left unnumbered it will be obvious that it derives from the same source as a larger quotation in its neighbourhood.

1. *Autobiographies*, p. 46.
2. Unpublished letter to Dowden, 8 Jan. 1884, quoted by Murphy in *Prodigal Father*, p. 124.
3. *Autobiographies*, p. 28.
4. *Ibid.*, p. 31.
5. *Ibid.*, p. 42.
6. Donoghue, ed., *W. B. Yeats: Memoirs*, p. 122.
7. *Autobiographies*, p. 44.
8. *Memoirs*, p. 19.
9. *Autobiographies*, p. 61.
10. *Mythologies*, p. 15.
11. *Autobiographies*, p. 60.
12. *Ibid.*, pp. 56-7.
13. *Ibid.*, pp. 58-9.
14. Sources for Yeats's time at the High School are Eglinton's essay in *The Dublin Magazine*, July-Sept. 1953 and *T. P.'s Weekly*, 7 June 1912 which contains 'Reminiscences of the Irish Poet's Schooldays' by the unnamed 'Classmate'.

15. *Autobiographies*, p. 83.
16. *Ibid.*, pp. 115-16.
17. See Ellmann, *Yeats: the Man and the Masks*, p. 47.
18. McHugh, ed., *Letters of Katharine Tynan to W. B. Yeats*, p. 11.
19. *Uncollected Prose*, Vol. I, pp. 81-104.
20. *Memoirs*, pp. 32-3.
21. *Ibid.*, p. 40.
22. *Ibid.*, p. 85.
23. *Autobiographies*, p. 182 *et seq.*
24. *Ibid.*, p. 337.
25. *Letters*, p. 340.
26. *Autobiographies*, p. 336.
27. *Samhain*, Dublin, Oct. 1901.
28. Lady Gregory, *Our Irish Theatre*, pp. 20-21.
29. *Autobiographies*, p. 416.
30. Ure, *Yeats the Playwright*, p. 11.
31. See Touhy, *Yeats*, p. 90.
32. *Commentary on Yeats's Plays*, p. 30.
33. *Essays and Introductions*, p. 105.
34. Hone, *W. B. Yeats*, p. 205.
35. *Ibid.*, p. 218.
36. *Letters*, p. 610.
37. *Ibid.*, p. 613.
38. *Ibid.*, p. 675.
39. 'Vengeance on the murderers of Jacques Molay', a Masonic toast symbolising for Yeats 'those who labour for hatred', is a refrain in 'Meditations in Time of Civil War'. See his note in *Collected Poems*, p. 534.
40. Pearce, ed., *The Senate Speeches of W. B. Yeats*, p. 30. All quotations from the Senate speeches are from this source.
41. *Letters*, p. 698.
42. *Autobiographies*, p. 553.
43. Krause, *Seán O'Casey and his World*, p. 28.
44. See Tuohy, *op. cit.*, pp. 192-3.
45. *Letters*, p. 729.
46. *Ibid.*, p. 763.
47. Unterecker, ed., *Yeats and Patrick McCartan: A Fenian Friendship*, p. 343.
48. *Letters*, p. 793.
49. *Explorations*, p. 358.
50. *Ibid.*, p. 354.
51. *Ibid.*, p. 337.
52. *Letters*, p. 835.

53. *Ibid.*, p. 856.

[136] 54. Krause, *op. cit.*

55. 'Meru', *Collected Poems*, p. 333.

56. 'The Gyres', *Collected Poems*, p. 337.

57. *Autobiographies*, p. 123.

58. These words describe the ancient Knight in 'Out of the Rose', *Mythologies*, p. 157.

59. *Memoirs*, p. 159.

60. *Memoirs*, p. 160. This frank statement provides an interesting comment on those 'psychoanalytic' studies of Yeats's work by such writers as David Lynch and Brenda Webster proving *inter alia* a mysterious 'mother-fixation' on the poet's part for Lady Gregory. An extreme example of this approach is Brenda Webster's suggestion that Lady Gregory as 'educating and nurturing mother' actually 'taught Yeats to talk'. So much for the poet's arduous self-training in the Contemporary Club where at the age of twenty he tested himself against the most formidable orator in Ireland, when he 'braved Taylor again and again' and mastered him, ten years before he had even met Lady Gregory.

61. Bax, ed., *Florence Farr, Bernard Shaw, W. B. Yeats: Letters*, p. ix.

62. *Ibid.*, p. v.

63. *Ibid.*, p. 54.

64. *Yeats, Sligo and Ireland.*

65. *Essays and Introductions*, p. 239.

66. Murphy, *The Yeats Family and the Pollexfens of Sligo*, p. 43.

67. See Harper, *W. B. Yeats and W. T. Horton: Record of an Occult Friendship*, p. 43.

68. *Autobiographies*, p. 424.

69. *Memoirs*, p. 46.

70. 'Four Elegies' in Jeffares, ed., *Yeats, Sligo, Ireland*, p. 230.

Select Bibliography

In drawing up a select bibliography certain seminal works must receive special mention. While awaiting Roy Foster's offical biography of Yeats it must be noted that Joseph Hone's life of the poet has not been superseded. Indeed it will always retain its advantage of personal acquaintance between biographer and subject. Allan Wade's *Bibliography* is a foundation stone in Yeatsian scholarship, and his fine edition of the *Letters* remains indispensible until John Kelly's massive and impending *Collected Letters* appears in twelve volumes. The work of A. Norman Jeffares in *W. B. Yeats: Man and Poet, W. B. Yeats, A New Biography*, and in the *Commentaries* on the poetry and plays is an unfailing source of information and insight. Richard Ellmann's three major works, *The Man and the Masks, The Identity of Yeats* and *Eminent Domain* seem to grow in authority with the years. The patient work of George Mills Harper among the manuscripts and the occult areas of the published work has expanded dramatically our sense of Yeats as a thinker. W. M. Murphy's life of the elder Yeats in *Prodigal Father* is not only an invaluable source of knowledge on the poet's childhood and the family background but is also one of the great biographies of our time.

Secondary Sources and References

Anglo-Irish Literary Background

Boyd, Ernest, *Ireland's Literary Renaissance*, new edition, Allen Figgis, Dublin 1968

Cronin, Anthony, *Heritage Now: Irish Literature in the English Language*, Dingle, Brandon 1982

Eager, Alan, *A Guide to Irish Bibliographical Material*, London, Library Association 1980

Finneran, Richard, *Anglo-Irish Literature, a Review of Research*,
[138]   Modern Language Association 1976
Finneran, Richard, *Recent Research on Anglo-Irish Writers*,
          Modern Language Association, 1983
Harmon, Maurice, *Select Bibliography for the Study of Anglo-Irish Literature and its Backgrounds: An Irish Studies Handbook*, Dublin, Wolfhound 1977
Jeffares, A. Norman, *Anglo-Irish Literature*, London, Macmillan 1982
McHugh, Roger, and Maurice Harmon, *Anglo-Irish Literature*, Dublin, Wolfhound 1982
Martin, Augustine, *Anglo-Irish Literature*, Dublin, Department of Foreign Affairs 1980
Welch, Robert, *Irish Poetry from Moore to Yeats*, Gerrards Cross, Colin Smythe 1980

Works by W. B. Yeats

Autobiographies, London, Macmillan 1955
A Vision, Revised by the Author, London, Macmillan 1937
Collected Poems, London, Macmillan 1950
Collected Plays, London, Macmillan 1953
Mythologies, London, Macmillan 1959
(Editor), *Fairy and Folk Tales of Ireland* (containing *Fairy and Folk Tales of the Irish Peasantry* and *Irish Fairy Tales*), Gerrards Cross, Colin Smythe 1973
(Editor), *Representative Irish Tales*, Gerrards Cross, Colin Smythe 1979

Bax, Clifford, ed., *Florence Farr, Bernard Shaw, W. B. Yeats: Letters*, London, Home and Van Thal 1946
Bridge, Ursula, ed., *W. B. Yeats and T. Sturge Moore; their correspondence*, London, Routledge & Kegan Paul 1953
Donoghue, Denis, ed., *Memoirs*, London, Macmillan 1972
Finneran, Richard, ed., *John Sherman and Dhoya*, Detroit, Wayne State University Press 1969
Frayne, John P., ed., *Uncollected Prose of W. B. Yeats*, London, Macmillan 1975
Frayne, John P. and Colton Johnson, eds, *Uncollected Prose of W. B. Yeats*, Vol. 2, London, Macmillan 1975

Gould, Warwick, Philip Marcus, and Michael J. Sidnell, eds, *The Secret Rose Stories*, Variorum edition, Ithica and London, Cornell University Press 1981

Harper, George Mills, and Walter K. Woods, eds, *A Vision (1925)*, Critical edition, London, Macmillan 1978

Jeffares, A. Norman ed., *Yeats's Poems*, London, Macmillan 1989

Kelly, John S., ed., *The Collected Letters of W. B. Yeats*, Vol. 1, 1865–1895, Oxford, Oxford University Press 1986

McHugh, Roger, ed., *Ah, Sweet Dancer: W. B. Yeats — Margot Ruddock, a Correspondence*, London, Macmillan 1970

McHugh, Roger, ed., *Letters of W. B. Yeats to Katharine Tynan*, Dublin, Clonmore and Reynolds; London, Burns, Oates and Washbourne 1953

O'Donnell, William H., ed., *The Speckled Bird*, Vols I and II, Dublin, Cuala Press 1973, 1974

Pearce, Donald R., ed., *The Senate Speeches of W. B. Yeats*, London, Faber and Faber 1961

Unterecker, John, ed., *Yeats and Patrick McCartan: a Fenian Friendship*, Dublin, Dolmen Press 1967

Wade, Allan, ed., *Letters of W. B. Yeats*, London, Macmillan 1954

Worth, Katharine, (ed.) *Where There is Nothing* and *The Unicorn from the Stars*, Washington DC, Catholic University of America Press, and Gerrards Cross, Colin Smythe 1987

Specialist Yeats Studies

Adams, Hazard, *Blake and Yeats: the contrary vision*, Ithaca, Cornell University Press 1955

Bloom, Harold, *Yeats*, New York, Oxford University Press 1970

Costello, Peter, *The Heart Grown Brutal*, Dublin, Gill and Macmillan 1977

Cullingford, Elizabeth, *Yeats, Ireland and Fascism*, Dublin, Gill and Macmillan 1981

Donoghue, Denis, *Yeats*, London, Fontana/Collins 1971

Ellmann, Richard, *Yeats, the Man and the Masks*, London, Macmillan 1949

Ellmann, Richard, *The Identity of Yeats*, London, Faber and Faber 1965

[140] Ellmann, Richard, *Eminent Domain*, New York, Oxford University Press 1967

Farag, Fahmy, *The Opposing Virtues*, Dublin, Dolmen Press 1974

Fay, Gerard, *The Abbey Theatre*, London, Hollis and Carter 1958

Flannery, James, *W. B. Yeats and the Idea of a Theatre*, Toronto, Macmillan 1976

Freyer, Grattan, *W. B. Yeats and the Anti-Democratic Tradition*, Dublin, Gill and Macmillan 1981

Gibbon, Monk, *The Masterpiece and the Man*, London, Rupert Hart-Davis 1959

Gregory, Augusta, Lady, ed., *Ideals in Ireland*, London, Unicorn 1901

Gregory, Augusta, Lady, *Seventy Years*, Gerrards Cross, Colin Smythe 1974

Gregory, Augusta, Lady, *Journals*, ed. Daniel J. Murphy, Vol. 1 (Books 1–29), Vol. 2 (Books 30–44), Gerrards Cross, Colin Smythe 1978 1987

Harper, George Mills, *Yeats's Golden Dawn*, New York, Barnes and Noble 1974

Harper, George Mills, *W. B. Yeats and W. T. Horton: a record of an occult friendship*, London, Macmillan 1980

Henn, T. R., *The Lonely Tower*, London, Methuen 1965

Jeffares, A. Norman, *W. B. Yeats, Man and Poet*, London, Routledge & Kegan Paul 1949

Jeffares, A. Norman, *A Commentary on the Collected Poems of W. B. Yeats*, London, Macmillan 1968

Jeffares, A. Norman, ed., *Yeats, Sligo and Ireland*, Gerrards Cross, Colin Smythe 1980

Jeffares, A. Norman, and A. S. Knowland, *A Commentary on the Collected Plays of W. B. Yeats*, London, Macmillan 1975

Jeffares, A. Norman, *A New Commentary on the Poems of W. B. Yeats*, London, Macmillan 1984

Jeffares, A. Norman, *W. B. Yeats, A New Biography*, London, Hutchinson 1988

Jeffares, A. Norman, ed., *Yeats the European*, Gerrards Cross, Colin Smythe 1989

Kiberd, Declan, *Synge and the Irish Language*, London, Macmillan 1979

Kilroy, James, *The Playboy Riots*, Dublin, Dolmen Press 1971

Krause, David, *Sean O'Casey and his World*, London, Thames [141] and Hudson 1976

Kuch, Peter, *Yeats and AE, the antagonism that unites dear friends*, Gerrards Cross, Colin Smythe 1986

Levine, Bernard, *The Dissolving Image*, Detroit, Wayne State University Press 1970

Lynch, David, *The Poetics of the Self*, University of Chicago Press 1979

Lyons, F. S. L., *Ireland Since the Famine*, London, Fontana 1973

Lyons, F. S. L., *Culture and Anarchy in Ireland 1890–1939*, Oxford, Oxford University Press 1979

Miller, Liam, *The Noble Drama of W. B. Yeats*, Dublin, Dolmen Press 1977

Moore, Virginia, *The Unicorn*, New York, Macmillan 1954

Murphy, William M., *Prodigal Father*, Ithaca and London, Cornell University Press 1978

O'Connor, Ulick, *Oliver St John Gogarty*, London, Jonathan Cape 1964

O hAodha, Micheal, *Theatre in Ireland*, Oxford, Basil Blackwell 1974

Saddlemyer, Ann, *Theatre Business, The Correspondence of the First Abbey Theatre Directors, W. B. Yeats, Lady Gregory and J. M. Synge*, Gerrards Cross, Colin Smythe 1982

Saddlemyer, Ann, and Colin Smythe, eds, *Lady Gregory, Fifty Years After*, Gerrards Cross, Colin Smythe 1987

Smythe, Colin, *A Guide to Coole Park, House of Lady Gregory*, 2nd ed., Gerrards Cross, Colin Smythe, 1983

Stallworthy, John, *Between the Lines*, Oxford, Oxford University Press 1963

Stallworthy, John, *Vision and Revision in Yeats's Last Poems*, Oxford, Oxford University Press 1969

Stock, A. G., *W. B. Yeats: his Poetry and Thought*, Cambridge University Press 1961

Torchiana, Donald, *Yeats and Georgian Ireland*, Oxford University Press 1966

Tuohy, Frank, *Yeats*, Dublin, Gill and Macmillan 1976

Unterecker, John, *A Reader's Guide to W. B. Yeats*, New York, Noonday 1959

[142]

Ure, Peter, *Yeats the Playwright*, London, Routledge & Kegan Paul 1963

Vendler, Helen Hennessy, *Yeats's Vision and the Later Plays, Cambridge, Massachusetts, Harvard University Press 1963*

Webster, Brenda, Yeats, a Psychoanalytic study, London, Macmillan 1973

Whitaker, Thomas R., *Swan and Shadow*, Chapel Hill, University of Carolina Press 1964

Wilson, F. A. C., *W. B. Yeats and Tradition*, London, Gollancz 1958

Wilson, F. A. C., *Yeats's Iconography*, London, Gollancz 1960

Yeats Annual, vols. 1–2 ed. Richard J. Finneran, vols. 3– ed. Warwick Gould, London, Macmillan 1982–

Yeats: An Annual of Critical and Textual Studies, ed. Richard J. Finneran, Ithaca, Cornell University Press 1983–85, then Ann Arbor, U.M.I. Research Press 1986–

NOTE ON THE GYRES

NOTE ON THE GYRES

The elaborate system of gyres, historical cycles, phases of the moon, divine incarnations, Magnus Annus and the Platonic Year constitute a field of study in itself. The simple sketch of the historical gyres offered here is especially adapted to a coherent reading of the poems. As the gyres change at the end of each epoch there is always violence. At each of these reversals there is, on the sketch, an exemplary poem, a personage, and a city or polity.

As far as the poems are concerned everything begins with the rape of Leda by Zeus, chief of the Olympian gods, bringing about the fall of Troy; a primary civilisation collapses at the moment of its greatest extension, and declines over 500 years. Meanwhile the antithetical tincture expands to produce the high civilisation of Athens, epitomised by the sculptor, Phidias. Another poem relevant to this phase is 'Nineteen Hundred and Nineteen'.

The primary tincture reaches a new culmination 500 years later with Christ, and the fall of Jerusalem, dramatised by Yeats's play *The Resurrection* and its 'Two Songs'. Christ sponsored a dispensation which demanded the primary virtues of discipline, obedience, conformity and reason. These qualities were transfigured, in Yeats's view, by the 'Unity of Being' of Byzantium five centuries later, with the antithetical tincture in the ascendant. The phase is celebrated in the two great Byzantium poems.

The rise of the new gyre reaches to 'world-transforming Charlemagne' of 'Supernatural Songs' and the rigid polity of the Middle Ages. The phase is most starkly dramatised in Yeats's story of medieval Ireland, 'the Crucifixion of the Outcast'. Antithetical Unity of Being is recovered 500 years later in the Renaissance glory of Castiglione's Urbino, celebrated in a series of poems on the patronage of art which include 'To a Wealthy Man' and 'To a Shade'.

The historical Gyres from Troy (1000 BC) to the New Bethlehem (2500 AD)

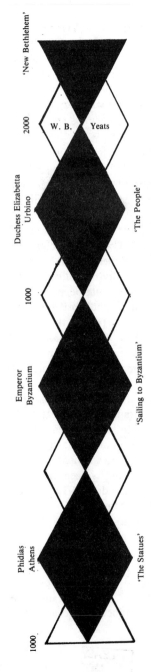

The Ebb and Flow of the Antithetical Tincture (Black)

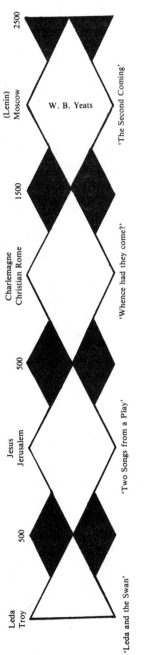

The Ebb and Flow of the Corresponding Primary Tincture (white)

The next primary phase is reaching its end when Yeats is born. He is forced to live his life fighting for the role of poetry, art and theatre. His sense of apocalypse grows with the rise of violence in Ireland and Europe in the second decade of the century, culminating in the Russian Revolution of 1917, the proximate occasion of 'The Second Coming' in which his visionary terrorism is most urgent. 'Meditations in Time of Civil War', 'The Gyres', 'Hound Voice' and 'A Bronze Head' are further witness to his mood. These chilling images are not visions of the coming polity or regime — i.e. Fascism, Communism — but traditional portents of change, of the primary gyre's implosion.

Out of this violence will emerge the new antithetical age, reaching its climax in 2500 AD. Yeats has no name for this high civilisation, so I will call it tentatively the 'New Bethlehem' — taking a hint from the last line of 'The Second Coming' — to complete the projected pattern. There is no reason to believe that this new epoch will not be as rich and imaginative as its great predecessors, Athens, Byzantium, Urbino. The gloomiest of Yeats's visions have within them, therefore, the promise of their defeat and transformation.

Index